Chaplain at War

KENNETH OLIVER

Angel Press

First published by Angel Press
Chichester, West Sussex, 1986
Reprinted 1988

British Library Cataloguing in Publication Data

Oliver, Kenneth
Chaplain at War.
1. Great Britain. *Army* – Chaplains
2. World War, 1939–1945 – Personal
narratives, British 3. World War, 1939–
1945 – Campaigns – Africa, North
I. Title
940.54′23′0924 D766.86

ISBN 0–947785–12–4

Photoset in Baskerville by
Northern Phototypesetting Co., Bolton
Printed in Great Britain by Hollen Street Press
and produced by Deer Park Productions, UK.

In loving memory of my mother

In gratitude to my wife, Anne

And in deep admiration for my friends and comrades in the 11th (HAC) RHA, especially those who did not return.

Contents

Foreword

I have read every word of the manuscript of this book with deep appreciation and with ever-increasing admiration for its author. For over fifty years it has been my privilege to claim friendship with this remarkable man; but the experience of reading this short autobiography has deepened my awareness of his qualities. Here is the story of a young parson whose life (like mine) was influenced by three outstanding personalities – Arthur Burroughs, who became Bishop of Ripon; Tubby Clayton, the Founder/Patron of Toc H; and B. K. Cunningham, Principal of Westcott House Theological College in Cambridge.

As a result of meeting these men, Ken Oliver was ordained. After two brief curacies, he became a Chaplain in Toc H. From there he joined the Royal Army Chaplains' Department in which he rose to the rank of Assistant Chaplain–General.

This book relates to a few years in his life and remarkable ministry – years in which he served as Chaplain for the most part to the HAC, serving in England, North Africa, Italy, Germany and the Far East.

As one reads this book, two words stand out – involvement and compassion. Here is a chaplain who is not merely concerned with men's souls. He is concerned with their bodies, their environment, their leisure time and their total well-being. In this involvement he makes use of all the talents which God has given him – his athletic prowess, his ability to act and to play in a danceband, and to organise. He does not "thrust religion down men's throats," but he is always "standing on the Godward side of men," ready to listen to their problems, to share their joys and sorrows and to introduce them to Christ, not just by words, but by the quality of his life. Many hundreds of men must have been attracted to Our Lord by the character and quiet witness of Kenneth Oliver.

The other word which stands out on almost every page is the word compassion – a word which in Latin and Greek means "suffering with". The author of this book has that rare and precious ability to suffer with and alongside the wounded, the dying and the bereaved. Here is one's ideal of an Army Chaplain.

I would like to see this book as compulsory reading for every young man who is thinking of joining any of the three chaplaincy departments. Indeed it would be of great benefit to any ordinand, while equally it could be a great source of refreshment to any priest or layman who has lost his way in the forest of chores or administration.

I am deeply grateful for this book and to its author. May it be widely read.

+ Cuthbert Bardsley

Acknowledgements

I would like to thank the following for their help:– my longstanding friend Bishop Cuthbert Bardsley, for writing the foreword; Angela Gibbs, for transforming my ghastly hand-writing into a readable typescript; and Michael and Janet Aldridge, for their unfailing encouragement, advice and support. I am also most grateful to Geoff Armstrong and Robin Smith, who read my manuscript and made most useful comments, and also to Mike Page, who allowed me to use a photograph from his extensive collection.

Origins of the Honourable Artillery Company

In 1537, King Henry VIII granted a charter to the Guild of St George, which eventually became known as the Honourable Artillery Company (HAC).

The origins of the Guild are not known but they quite clearly go back to the Middle Ages. The members were originally archers and they acted as trained bands in the city of London. Their pikemen still accompany the Lord Mayor on his ceremonial occasions.

They played a notable part in the army that was hastily organised to defend England against the threat of the Armada in 1588.

During the Civil War, although a number of them fought for the King, the majority of them formed the basis of the trained bands of the City that checked the Royalists at Turnham Green and defeated them at the Battle of Newbury under the leadership of the renowned soldier Philip Skippon.

During the centuries that followed, many members of the Company became regular soldiers, while the company itself was always available to keep order in the city at times of civil disturbance.

During the Boer War the company provided a battery with the City Imperial Volunteers that fought in South Africa.

In the 1914 War, they provided four Horse Artillery

Batteries and two Infantry Battalions all of whom fought overseas. In all, 14,000 men passed through the ranks of the regiment, winning three VC's and a very large number of other decorations for gallantry.

In between the wars, the regiment became an officer-producing establishment in addition to maintaining an Infantry Battalion and two batteries of Horse Artillery.

During the 1939 War, the regiment provided 3,800 commissioned officers who served with almost every unit of the army, including a number with the Navy and the RAF.

In addition, the 11th, 12th and 13th RHA were largely HAC regiments, as was the 86th HAA (Heavy Anti-Aircraft). A great number of decorations including the VC were won by members of the regiment, and 723 were killed in action.

HM The Queen is the Captain-General of the regiment and the Vellum Book contains the signatures of many reigning monarchs from Charles II onwards. Recent Colonel Commandants include Lord Gort and Field-Marshal Alanbroke.

The regiment maintains a regular contact with the Ancient and Honourable Artillery Company of Massachusetts formed by members of the regiment in 1637. Regular visits are exchanged both in England and America.

Prologue

As he climbed up into the pulpit, the preacher did not look a very impressive figure. He was a small slight man with a rather large head. But once he began to preach, his personality seemed to expand, and he demanded a hearing.

His theme was Parsifal and the search for the Holy Grail, the most sacred thing in the world, and I listened spellbound. At the end of the service, the headmaster said that if anyone wished to meet the preacher, he would be in his study.

At the age of sixteen, the headmaster's study at Christ's Hospital was not a place to enter without being sent for, but I felt I must go. I persuaded my great friend, Charlie Jennings, to accompany me, and together we called on the preacher. He was Arthur Burroughs, Dean of Bristol, and he remained a great influence in my life until he died ten years later at the age of fifty-three. He had worn himself out in the service of his Master.

During those ten years, he convinced me that the highest form of service to God and man was to become a clergyman. I was rather reluctant. The image of a parson did not inspire me; also, I knew I was not good enough and I felt it might inhibit me from doing many things I enjoyed doing and, in some way, cut me off from my fellow men, but Arthur Burroughs never let go. He had a wonderful gift of inspiring young men and he made me feel that no other job was really worthwhile.

In spite of a number of setbacks, mostly academic, as I was much keener on rugger and cricket and other sports than on the pursuit of learning, I eventually managed to satisfy the examiners of Oxford University, and emerged with a degree. My final training had to be at a theological college and this might well have been a real stumbling block. After the rather carefree life of an undergraduate, eighteen months at a theological college seemed rather daunting, and I suspect that had I gone to a more conventional college, I would have found the regime too restrictive and would have failed to last the pace. However, one or two of my Oxford friends came back from a visit to Cambridge with the news that they had met a most remarkable man, Canon B. K. Cunningham, who was principal of a theological college called Westcott House, and this was where I finally went. It was a most wonderful experience.

B. K. Cunningham displayed, more than almost anyone else I ever met, the naturalness and joy of the Christian faith. Although almost completely deaf, he inspired all his students with a deep affection for himself and the certainty that we were in the presence of a saint, but a perfectly human saint. One of them once said, "I suppose he has his faults, but I am damned if I know what they are." B.K. developed at Westcott House an atmosphere that was unique amongst theological colleges. He refused to be tied to any party line and welcomed men of diverse churchmanship. He was a supreme example of the comprehensiveness of the Church of England. He was determined to preserve what was natural and human in those he was training to become parsons. He believed that the rather old-fashioned qualities of an English gentleman were still required by the Church, and that good manners, combined with a sense of humour and fun, were all part and parcel of being a Christian minister.

There was a minimum of rules and regulations, but great stress was laid on what was called "the common life." This was the tradition of self-discipline that everyone contributed to the house. I thrived under these conditions and was confirmed in my view that the Christian ministry was a great challenge and a high vocation.

During the winter I was still allowed to play rugger for the Old Blues, although this often meant being away for the whole of Saturday. In the summer, we ran our own cricket team and played many delightful matches in neighbouring villages, with B.K. in the team.

I spent a very happy eighteen months at Westcott House and managed to pass the necessary exams to qualify me for ordination.

I still had doubts about my vocation. I knew that I would never be good enough in my personal life and, although I had moments when the presence of God seemed very real, there were other moments when I felt I was being rather a hypocrite and very conscious of my lack of real devotion. I also still rather shuddered at the thought of wearing a clerical collar and marking myself off from my fellow men.

Arthur Burroughs, then Bishop of Ripon, had kept in touch with me throughout this time and invited me to serve in his diocese. This was quite in line with B.K.'s wishes, as he always hoped that those of us who had been brought up in the more prosperous parts of the South of England would volunteer for service in the industrial North. Before my ordination, he invited me to stay with him in his palace at Ripon. He was an easy man to talk to and I was able to express my doubts before taking the final irrevocable step. He was most sympathetic and understanding. He told me that no one thought he was good enough to become a parson, and that serving God in that way did not mean he felt he was better than other people. The important thing was to feel that God was calling him to serve in this particular way and to know that he could rely on God to give him the strength to overcome his human weaknesses. As St Paul wrote in his letter to the Thessalonians, "He is faithful who called you." The bishop said, "It is not a question of being good enough, but simply of knowing that God was calling." My doubts were finally overcome when I attended a Communion service in the palace chapel. The sun was shining through the east window; I heard the bishop say, "God so loved the world that he gave His only begotten son . . ." I knew then I must go forward to ordination.

I was sent to a parish in Leeds called Roundhay. It was 1932, a time of great depression in the North, and much unemployment. In many parts of Leeds there were Unemployment Centres supported by the Church, where men were encouraged to help each other by using their skills for the benefit of the community. I visited one of these centres regularly and became convinced that my vocation in the Christian ministry was to work amongst men.

An added delight in my parish was to find an excellent rugby team and a vicar who encouraged me to play every Saturday. After completing my first curacy in Leeds, I was offered a second curacy in Birmingham, where I would be in charge of a small mission church in a new housing area. The idea was to build a permanent church on the site and combine it with a church hall. We managed to complete this project while I was there.

I was very fortunate in having another most kindly and sympathetic vicar, Reg Tait. He was a bachelor and a scholar, a great student of English literature. It was most fitting that, after leaving Birmingham, he became vicar of Grasmere, the parish where William Wordsworth wrote many of his poems. I spent many pleasant holidays in the vicarage at Grasmere and soon learnt to have a great love for the Lakes and their countryside.

While I was in Birmingham, I made contact with a

branch of Toc H, and although it was not in my parish, I was invited to become their chaplain. In those days, Toc H was largely a men's society although it had a League of Women Helpers attached to most branches. I had come across Tubby Clayton, the founder padre of Toc H, both at school and at University, and had been greatly taken with him.

Tubby Clayton was one of the outstanding priests in the Church of England during the first part of the twentieth century. He had a supreme gift for friendship and always managed to see in quite ordinary people qualities of great worth and loveliness. In building Toc H in the early twenties he gathered around him a number of men of great ability from many different walks of life. He was no administrator but he found in Peter Monie, who had just retired from the Indian Civil Service, and Hubert Secretan, who had been prominent in the Ministry of Shipping during the war, two first-class administrators who laid the foundations on which the organisation of Toc H was built.

Tubby provided the inspiration. He was essentially a man of prayer and he conducted the Eucharist in a way that was unique and full of inspiration. I have never forgotten assisting him in a service of Holy Communion in 1938 in the little chapel that had been constructed out of a hop-loft in the Old House at Poperinghe where Toc H was born. He was quite clearly absorbed by the memory of the hundreds of soldiers who had worshipped with him during the 1914 war and had gone from the service to their deaths in the trenches. He made the Communion of Saints an absolute reality. Wonderful knowledge and love of the Bible was combined with a gift of imparting that love to others. These great spiritual qualities were combined with a deep humility and an impish sense of humour. His friendship was a gift and an inspiration for which I shall be always grateful.

Tubby Clayton had made a great contribution to the

welfare of soldiers behind the line at Poperinghe in the 1914 war. He had set up a club where all ranks could go and find refreshment and recreation. What made it different from other such clubs, was first, in the personality of Tubby himself; secondly, that officers and men could mix freely; and thirdly, in the spiritual atmosphere generated from the chapel in the hop-loft at the top of the house that became known as "the Upper Room". So great was the impact made on many hundreds of soldiers, that, at the end of the war, there was a great demand that the fellowship formed during those ghastly years of fighting, should not be allowed to die. Thus, Toc H was formed, to carry into peacetime the spirit of fellowship, service and spiritual power that so many men discovered in the horror of trench warfare.

When I joined the Toc H staff in London in 1936, there were over one hundred flourishing branches in London and many others all over the British Isles and the countries of the Commonwealth. Thus, I was highly delighted when I was invited to join the Toc H staff in London. Many of my church friends were not keen about my taking this step. My first vicar said that I was committing "ecclesiastical suicide." He regarded Toc H as being outside the mainstream of church life.

Tubby Clayton had been appointed Vicar of All Hallows, by the Tower of London, and this had become the Guild Church of Toc H. I was responsible for over fifty branches in South London, and was also an assistant priest at All Hallows church. I found in Toc H a practical application of the Christian faith which cut across barriers of class and religious denomination. It was an exhilarating experience and gave me a breadth of vision rather wider than I had experienced in parish life. It also confirmed my belief that my vocation in the Church was to work amongst men.

It was now becoming fairly certain that another war was likely to break out before very long. Like many of my contemporaries, I wondered whether, as a Christian, I ought to become a pacifist. War was quite clearly contrary to the Will of God and a Christian minister should surely be a man of peace. Ought I to stand aside if my country went to war and the great majority of my contemporaries were serving in the forces of the Crown? I decided I could not stand aside and that if my services were required as a chaplain, I must go. War was evil, but submitting to a tyranny that threatened to enslave the whole of Europe was a far worse evil. The example of Tubby Clayton, and many splendid Christians who had ministered to men in the trenches and on the high seas, confirmed my determination that my duty would be to take my place alongside the men of my generation and to attempt to bring the Church to them in the midst of all the horror and destruction of war.

Chapter One

Joining Up

It was almost by chance that I became an army chaplain. My brothers were both in the navy, and before I was ordained I was interviewed, along with Jack Holland, by the Archdeacon of the Fleet and put provisionally on the list of the Naval Reserve of Chaplains.

Jack Holland and I had been together both at St Edmund Hall and Westcott House. As well as being fellow theological students, we shared an enthusiasm for rugger and cricket, and during our student days, played together at both sports. We had an amusing rivalry at cricket. Jack was essentially a wicket-keeper and I was mostly a bowler. We both rather fancied our batting and had a constant rivalry as to who would bat first, usually at number seven or eight in our college team. In our last year at Oxford, I had the unfair advantage of being captain of our college XI, and usually went in before him.

Jack went into the navy as a regular chaplain and had a distinguished career over twenty-five years. We still meet at regular intervals.

When I was working with Tubby Clayton of Toc H in London, one day in 1938 he said to me, "Ken, old boy, I have been asked by Brian Dickson whether I could suggest a chaplain for the Honourable Artillery Company. Would you like to go and see whether you would suit them?"

I had no idea what the Honourable Artillery Company

was, but when Tubby Clayton assured me they were a "grand bunch of chaps," I naturally agreed to try. I was invited by the Second-in-Command, Major Jack Hill, to meet Colonel Goldsworthy for lunch at St Stephen's Club at Westminster. The colonel was a formidable veteran from the first war and a real Colonel Blimp. When I told him that my father had been killed in the battle of the Somme and that both my brothers were serving in the Royal Navy, he seemed to think that I might fit into the HAC. So I became their chaplain and soon realised how true Tubby Clayton's words were when he said they were a "grand bunch of chaps." I am still their chaplain, forty-eight years later, and am eternally grateful for all the friends that I have made during those years.

When war broke out in 1939, I remembered that I was still on the list of Naval Reserve of Chaplains and wondered what I should do about it. When I went to Armoury House to discuss my dilemma, the first man I met was the Regimental Sergeant-Major. When I explained my quandary he said, "Don't worry about that padre, you're in the army." I discovered that, with the whole Territorial Army, the HAC had been embodied into the regular army and that I had become an Army Chaplain! I remained an Army Chaplain for twenty-one years and never regretted a moment of it.

I was soon summoned to appear before the Assistant Chaplain-General of Southern Command. He appeared rather surprised when I said I had joined the HAC. "Oh no," he said, "you have joined the Royal Army Chaplains' Department." When I humbly suggested that I rather hoped to spend the war with the HAC, he replied that I might stay with them for the moment, but I must be prepared to go wherever the Chaplains' Department ordered me.

I was lucky enough to stay with the HAC for another three years, until I was promoted Senior Chaplain, and I never served with another regiment. Senior Chaplains are usually posted to a division.

On the day war was declared, I travelled up to London to report at Armoury House. I arrived at Holborn Station just as all the sirens sounded, announcing an imminent air raid. All traffic came to a halt but, as I was walking towards Moorgate, a milk van was hurrying down City Road. I hailed the milkman and was given a lift and thus arrived in state at Armoury House! Slit trenches had been dug on the sports field and everyone had taken refuge in them, complete with gas masks. The 'all clear' was soon sounded and we retired to the Sutling Room for a pre-lunch drink. The war had begun.

After a few days, we were posted to our first war station at Elstree. Sadly, the Infantry Battalion was refused the opportunity of serving as a regiment adding to the honours it had won in the 1914–1918 war. They marched through the city on their way to Aldershot where they formed the 162 (HAC) OCTU from where, eventually, hundreds of officers were despatched to almost every unit and branch of the army and added to the great number of awards for gallantry won by the HAC gunner regiments in the war.

I was attached to what was now known as the 11th (HAC) Regiment RHA, and I also had responsibility for our second regiment, the 12th (HAC) RHA, who were posted in the neighbouring locality of Boreham Wood amongst the Elstree Film Studios. These two regiments were the senior territorial regiments of the Royal Regiment of Artillery.

The 11th at Elstree Village was billeted in a number of private houses, some evacuated and some still occupied by their owners. I was lucky enough to be billeted, along with the colonel and most of the officers of RHQ, with a delightful elderly couple, Mr and Mrs Wellington, who were most charming hosts. I remember sitting down to an enormous breakfast consisting of eggs, sausages and bacon, with a selection of cold meats and fish as an alternative or an addition. The austerity of rationing had not yet begun!

'A' Battery were fortunate enough to have taken over the well-known preparatory school at Elstree, whose pupils had been evacuated to the West country. The officers' mess was happily situated in the local pub where I spent many happy evenings. After one convivial party, I was not feeling at my best the next morning at breakfast, and I refused the offer of eggs, sausages and bacon, much to the amusement of my fellow officers. Mrs Wellington said, "Oh dear, the padre is not looking very well this morning." The colonel muttered, "I thought I saw him coming in rather late last night." Unfortunately, the room that I shared with the Medical Officer was next door to the colonel, and we had to creep past his room after a late night with the batteries.

Meanwhile, I was trying to learn the padre's job. My first responsibility was the weekly church parade, and while the weather remained fine, both regiments paraded in the extensive grounds of the Wellington's house. The 12th Regiment had to march up a rather steep hill from Boreham Wood and, many years after, I was to meet old members of the regiment. "Oh, I remember you, Padre, we had to march up the steep hill to attend your church parades!"

I was very conscious that church parades could be rather unpopular, especially when the men had been paraded under the vigilant eye of a fierce sergeant-major and addressed in language far from ecclesiastical! Before the first Sunday, the colonel sent for me on the Saturday morning and said, "Padre, about the church parade on Sunday. The sermon will last for seven and a half minutes!" I could only reply with the guardsmen's answer to a superior officer, "Sir," meaning "Yes Sir." He added with a twinkle, "The half-minute is a concession." Again, I could only answer, "Sir." It was actually very sound advice and I followed it precisely.

Soldiers who have been on parade for an hour or so, and remain standing during the whole service, do not relish a longer sermon. When the winter came and the church parades were in the local churches, the colonel allowed me ten minutes! I felt quite sure that with well-known hymns, relevant prayers and a short sermon, very few soldiers really disliked a church parade service. I also received a useful tip from the sergeant-major. "Padre, speak to the men in their own language." Those who have heard something of soldier's language will realise that this was a rather double-edged comment, but I realised what he meant: keep your sermons down to earth. Even if one was trying to draw the men to heaven, one was to use the language of the earth!

After the church parade in the morning, my duty in the afternoon was to keep the colonel amused! Colonel Goldsworthy was a large man with red hair and bushy eyebrows – a man of few words but of great presence. He was an enthusiastic territorial, but his ideas of military art were rather out-of-date. He was reputed to have landed at Gallipoli in the 1914–18 War, complete in full dress uniform and Spurs. He imagined he was a cross between Wellington and Napoleon, but his experience with a horsed battery of the City of London Yeomanry Territorials during the years of peace had not been a very good preparation to command a regiment of mechanised artillery in war. Although he was married, we never met his wife during the year in which he remained in command, as he was convinced that the presence of wives anywhere near the regiment would be the greatest handicap to our becoming an efficient regiment. This was not popular with the other married officers or with their wives!

When it became apparent that during what was called the 'phoney war' we were unlikely to go to Europe, it became more difficult for the colonel to keep the wives away from their husbands. He was also very reluctant to allow any member of the regiment to get married. Naturally, a number of men were engaged and hoping to get married before the regiment went abroad. I was often asked to intercede with the colonel to allow the potential bridegrooms enough leave to get married. My own batman-driver was one of these, and when I asked the colonel to grant him an extra day's leave to get married, he remarked, "What on earth does he want to get married for? Doesn't he realise there's a war on?", I found it difficult to give an adequate answer without offering the obvious comment that, even in war-time, life must go on.

On another occasion, I was going off to marry one of my fellow officers and I asked the colonel whether he would give me a message for the groom. "Yes, padre," he said, "you can tell him from me, he is an ass." That went down well at the reception, where the colonel's views on marriage were well known!

Another hilarious memory of this man was when we were finally posted to the seaside at Swanage. The colonel decreed that no one would be allowed to bathe before passing a swimming test. Arthur Green, the assistant adjutant, rowed him out in a very small dinghy, out of depth of a normal man. The colonel, who looked very large in this small boat, said that any man who could swim out and around the boat would pass the test. Unfortunately, like King Canute, he failed to realise that the tide was going out rather rapidly. By the time most of the men had passed the colonel's boat, they could swim with one foot on the ground, as the boat was in barely four feet of water. Thus, most of the troops were able to pass the swimming test without too much trouble and thus enjoy some sea bathing during the lovely but dramatic summer of 1940.

When the colonel was finally relieved of his command by a regular officer on the grounds of age and lack of war experience, we were sad to say goodbye to one who, in spite of his old-fashioned eccentricity, had endeared himself to us by his complete integrity, devotion to duty and his patriotism. I had lost a friend who had been a sympathetic guide and mentor to a very raw young chaplain.

He refused to retire into some safe post at home and volunteered for the position of OC Troops on troopships sailing to the Middle and Far East, always in danger from enemy submarines. On one occasion his ship was sunk and he spent a number of days in an open boat before being finally rescued. He was indeed brave and gallant and a splendid example of the best type of English gentleman.

In the early days of the war at Elstree, the regiment struggled with a number of conflicting roles. In the first place, we had to release any man still serving in the ranks who was assessed as a potential officer. A number had already departed, either to direct commissions or to various OCTU's. Their places had been taken by a number of volunteers, splendid young men, keen to join the army.

The colonel had been ordered to accept volunteers only of the best type of non-officer material. As an old Etonian and country squire, his idea of non-officer material was slightly old-fashioned and out of date. When the first selection board arrived to weed out potential officers, a very large proportion of our first batch of recruits were soon removed to be trained as officers. Our next batch was of a rather different quality. Soon after their arrival, money was stolen from the regimental mess funds. When the aid of the CID was reluctantly requested, they asked to see our latest batch of recruits. When these men had been seen, the inspector remarked to the colonel, "Many of these faces are rather familiar, most of them have just been discharged from Wormwood Scrubbs or Pentonville!" However, many of them remained with us and became first-class soldiers.

Having surrendered all the potential officers, our next

task was to mould our recruits into efficient gunners. Our future role was to be to support the 1st Armoured Division with two batteries of twenty-five pounder guns. During this time, we were given the task of sending various parties to guard vulnerable points in London, such as airfields, railway and river bridges, and other points of strategic importance. Equipment of all kinds, including uniforms, was slow to materialise, the winter was cold, and the sight of our men in Montague Burton overcoats was reminiscent of the "manning of the barricades."

In the midst of all this chaos, I was trying to find out what a chaplain was expected to do when his Sunday duties were over. I had had no training, apart from one territorial camp, and had been pitchforked straight from civilian life into the army. Chaplains who joined later were fortunate enough to be sent on training courses at Chester, and later Tidworth, before joining their first regiment. In fact, after the war, I was put in charge of a similar Chaplains' Training Centre at Bagshot Park, but that, as Kipling said, "was another story."

In the early days of the war I did not find it easy to adjust my thinking with regard to the role of a chaplain in the life of the regiment. Apart from doing one Territorial Summer camp with the regiment I received no guidelines as to what my duties might be during the week. My main task was to make friends with all ranks and to establish myself as a useful member of the regimental team.

There were a few churchmen who would welcome discussion groups and Bible study and a few who might be willing to join a confirmation class, but the majority were busily preparing for war and apart from attending church parades were not really concerned with the Christian faith. They did not resent the presence of a chaplain but could not really see much advantage of having one about. The navy had a very good description of their chaplain, he should be "the friend and adviser of all on board." I tried to adopt this as my theme song in the regiment.

I soon found that there were certain areas concerning the general welfare of the soldiers where the chaplain might be of use. As I got to know the battery and troop commanders they began to ask my advice about various matters concerning the family problems of their men. I soon found that all good officers were personally concerned with the welfare of their men, but every now and again came up against problems in which they felt out of their depth. As I gained the confidence of the officers I became more involved in these sort of problems.

I found that among many army chaplains there was a disinclination to get involved in any activities that were not specifically 'religious'. I felt on the contrary that I was concerned with every aspect of the soldier's life and that whatever abilities I had should be put at their disposal. Thus I found that a good deal of my time was taken up with running entertainments and taking part in games and sport. In this way I made friends with a number of soldiers who would never think of calling on my services as a clergyman.

All officers and men were extremely busy during the day and the constant influx of new recruits made it difficult to get to know the rank and file. One of the temptations of a chaplain, is to make friends with the officers, at the expense of getting to know the other ranks. A chaplain ranked as a captain and lived in the officers' mess, and was at first quite clearly regarded by the ordinary soldiers as just another officer. Things like weekday services, Bible classes and preparation for confirmation candidates were not easy to launch. I remember the remark of one very experienced chaplain, it may well have been Tubby Clayton himself, saying to me, "Don't worry too much if none of the soldiers appear to need your services as a parson. You will find that very few of them will not be prepared to regard you as a friend." I tried to work on these lines although there was always a nucleus of men who had been churchmen and welcomed the usual church activities.

Naturally I took a great interest in the training that was going on and I remember realising the way the guns were regarded in an artillery regiment when I attended an exercise and the adjutant said, "Ah, here come the guns." He stood to attention and almost saluted as they went by.

Every one of the 700 officers and men was largely concerned in getting the guns into action as soon as possible, although very few, including myself, would ever have the opportunity of firing them. This came to me with even greater emphasis when, in our first battle action, we lost several guns. It was regarded as a terrible disgrace.

I couldn't spend all my time wandering around watching other people work and make no real contribution. In spite of the fact that some soldier said that the padre had an easy job ("He was paid a pound a day for smiling!"), it seemed to me that I should try doing something more constructive than merely walking about and smiling!

There were, of course, visits to be made to men in hospital. This was not always easy as the hospital was some way off, and as at this stage we were very short of transport, the padre was the last person to have a car of his own. My only means of transport was a bicycle!

However, after a week or so of frustration, I had a piece of luck. I was invited to a dance at our headquarters, and while doing my duty with a very impressive looking dowager, she asked me how I enjoyed my work. I replied, that apart from the frustration of being unable to visit men in need, due to lack of transport, I was finding it most absorbing. "No transport," she almost shouted, "Why didn't you tell me before? I control a number of young women who have volunteered to drive their own cars in the service of their country. Let me know where you are billeted and I will send one down to you first thing in the morning."

Sure enough, at nine o'clock the next morning, a very smart sports car drove up to our billet and out stepped a most decorative young lady in some kind of uniform. Conscious that the colonel and other 'carless' officers were watching with amazement, I stepped out rather nervously to be greeted with a splendid salute and was ceremoniously ushered into the passenger seat. I easily imagined the comments from my fellow officers as we drove off in some style!

In spite of a good deal of leg-pulling, I was able to visit various hospitals and other out-lying units where some of our soldiers were. Sometimes I did not get the kind of reception I expected in hospital. One of the first men I visited, at the request of the orderly-room sergeant, was in a hospital some fifteen miles away. My glamorous driver turned up punctually and off we drove. When I found the ward where the soldier was lying, the sister pointed out his bed, and I made my way, thinking either he must be very seriously ill or he must want to have some religious conversation. As I approached his bed his eyes lit up. "Oh, Padre," he said, "I *am* glad to see you. I haven't had a smoke since I have been here. Could you get me a packet of fags?" It was hardly the question I was expecting but it made me realise that this recruit had picked out the padre as a friendly man in the midst of unfamiliar circumstances.

With my car and driver, I was able to visit small parties of men guarding 'vulnerable points' all over London and was beginning to make myself more useful. I was still pretty ignorant of many military matters and, from time to time, dropped some pretty hefty bricks! I was visiting one of our batteries who were guarding the aerodrome at Purley. After the guard-mounting, I remarked to the sergeant-major, who later became a very good friend, "Very smart turn-out Sergeant-Major." "Padre," he said, "this is no job for horse-artillery men." I began to glean something of the pride of the Royal Horse Artillery who exercised their privilege of always parading with their guns 'right of the line'.

As the new recruits came streaming in, I asked the adjutant whether I could have a short talk with all of them as they arrived. "Certainly Padre," he said, "you can have them after their medical." This was a great advantage as at least I could let the newcomers know that they had a chaplain at their disposal. It also gave me a chance of seeing the kind of men we were now getting and what their interests and abilities were likely to be.

I soon found a great ally in the adjutant; we were very fortunate in ours. Each territorial regiment had a regular adjutant to advise and assist the colonel, especially in matters of training. Richard Goodbody was one of the finest soldiers I ever had the honour of knowing. He was a captain when war broke out and had been with the regiment for some years before. It was rumoured that he had played a prominent part in persuading the powers that be that the HAC, in spite of being pledged to lose all its potential officers, could still play a useful part in the RHA and, with its great tradition, should not be deprived of the opportunity of winning battle honours in the war. Thus it was agreed that our numbers would be kept up with fresh drafts. In fact, a third HAC gunner regiment was formed, the 13th RHA.

Richard was an enthusiast in everything that he did, as well as being a dedicated and brilliant soldier. It was a tremendous asset to the regiment to have him in such a key position at a time when everything was in such a state of chaos. He always kept alive in us the final ideal of becoming worthy of the great traditions of the Royal Horse Artillery. He had that most unusual combination of great drive and great charm. We were all proud to have him as our friend and mentor. With the utmost tact he stood behind the colonel and treated him with the greatest respect, but we were all aware that he was the power behind the throne. Although he left us on promotion, after about six months, he made a great impact on us all and the whole regiment rejoiced when he returned in 1942 to take command at a time when things had not been going well.

He completed a distinguished career by becoming Adjutant General of the army and Colonel Commandant of the HAC. During the four hundred years of the regiment's history, no one ever made a greater contribution to its well-being than our beloved Richard Goodbody. He remained a lifelong friend of us all.

As the weeks of the 'phoney war' went by, I was beginning to find ways in which I could make myself useful and, at the same time, become an integral part of the regiment. Most of the new recruits were far from physically fit, and when they joined, the colonel asked whether I knew anything about PT. As I was still playing fairly strenuous games, I reckoned I was pretty fit myself having, during the past, often taken part in Physical Training exercises. I volunteered to take a batch of recruits in some preliminary exercises, and until we had a full trained PT instructor posted to us, I found myself in charge of all recruits for PT. Out of this we began to organise games of rugger and football and to my delight I found we had a number of very useful players. As I was still playing for the Old Blues in the London Season at the outbreak of war, I found myself appointed captain of the team, as well as being match secretary, which meant getting in touch with what London clubs were still functioning, and arranging fixtures. We had a most unforgettable and enjoyable season, and as far as I remember, were unbeaten, including a win over my old club, the Old Blues. One of our most exciting games was against our second line, the 12th RHA, who were also unbeaten. After a very stirring battle, we just managed a victory and, I may add that I won a small bet, half-a-crown, with their colonel.

Another activity in which I found myself involved, was entertainment. We were out in the wilds at Elstree and the local pub was about the only form of entertainment in the evening. The colonel asked whether I could find any variety stars who would come and do a show for the troops. I was fairly successful, as the theatrical world was rather upside down, and many well-known performers were most generous in giving their services free. They obviously regarded it as their contribution to the war effort. Later, an official organisation was founded. Naturally, some of the shows were fairly vulgar, to say the least, sometimes slightly embarrassing, when the organiser was the chaplain! I remember a sister act called the Huston Sisters, who were a very well-known, if slightly risqué variety turn. After a series of fairly rude jokes, Renee Huston, the leading sister, spotted me in the front row feeling rather self-conscious in my clerical collar. "Hello Padre," she said. "Are you still here? At the last show I gave I had the chaplain out of the hall after half-an-hour!" The soldiers enjoyed that very much!

As the supply of outside entertainers gradually ran out, I realised we had a good deal of potential among us. When I interviewed the recruits I always enquired after their interests and talents. It soon became apparent that we could establish a concert party of our own. As I was beginning to see the possibilities of this development, an extremely talented amateur entertainer joined us. Basil Green had been a member of the Gang Show, a concert party formed out of the Boy Scout Movement, organised and produced by Ralph Reader, who was a highly professional theatrical producer. These shows were produced annually and had been running with great success for a number of years.

Basil had been assistant producer to Ralph Reader, and as in those days it was a completely male company, he was ideally suited to be producer of a regimental concert party. In additon to that, he had access to all the material the Gang Show had used with great success: sketches, songs, choruses, playlets and many other useful items of entertainment. We soon gathered together a number of volunteers and started rehearsing energetically.

Before long we produced our first concert and from then, until we went abroad, we nearly always had our entertainment on the stocks. Apart from the Gang Show material, we discovered several individual performers with considerable talent. Among them was our regimental quarter-master, a great character and one of the veteran members of the regiment. Leycester Bedwell was a member of the Stock Exchange in peace time and, in his younger days, had been one of the regimental trumpeters. He was a prominent member of the Stock Exchange Dramatic Society and was a born comic with a dry sense of humour, rather in the style of Buster Keaton.

His favourite turn was a recital of Stanley Holloway's famous monologues about Sam and his musket and little Albert and the lion. He was also an excellent female impersonator, in the style of the pantomime dame. Another individual turn was based on one of the most famous European clowns who did a variety of sketches varying from a football goalkeeper to a lady undressing in a bath. This was Gunner L.W. Rotger, who in peace-time became a member of the Company of Pikemen. Robin Smith was once his replacement and performed with great success.

We also discovered a very clever conjurer whose favourite turns were swallowing razor blades and borrowing pound notes from members of the audience, putting them in an envelope and apparently setting fire to them. The first night he performed this trick, he managed to persuade the colonel, sitting in the front row, to hand him the pound note. The troops cheered as it was apparently set on fire, much to the colonel's fury. However, all ended well as the pound was discovered buried in an orange held by another member of the audience. It was rather messy when it was finally returned to the colonel.

One of the problems of running a regimental concert party was the matter of duties and guards, to say nothing of having vital members of the cast confined to barracks and unable to travel with the party. On one ghastly occasion, my producer Basil Green was given CB on the night of the final dress rehearsal before a very vital performance. I remember calling on the assistant adjutant, Peter Sworder, fully dressed in my clerical robes, to demand his release. We managed to come to some reasonable compromise, but the adjutant pulled my leg afterwards by saying, "I knew I was in for trouble when the padre arrived in my office fully dressed in his ceremonials!" This was the beginning of a lifelong friendship.

I had to be prepared to understudy any member of the cast who happened to be away on duty. One of our most popular turns was a song entitled "I wonder how my Willie's getting on." Three soldiers, disguised as elderly mothers, arrive in camp to find out what has happened to their dear sons. More than once, I had to dress myself up and take the part of one of the mothers, owing to the non-appearance of the regular performer who had been given some extra duty. However, it was all great fun and the concert party performed regularly wherever we were stationed, both to the troops and to civilian audiences.

An important event for me in the early days, was the arrival of Henry Andrews, henceforth known as Andy. It was quite clear that unless I took some steps in the matter, I would be alloted a batman-driver who might be unsuitable and out of sympathy with my work as a chaplain. I really needed someone I could rely on as a friend and a Christian.

I rang up one of my old Toc H friends, Bill Harris, whom I knew had a number of very fine young men in his Toc H branch at Mitcham. I asked him if he had anyone who might be willing to join the regiment as my batman. When the time came that I was given a vehicle of my own, he would be promoted to batman-driver. After some careful thought he said that one of his best members was a young man called Andrews, who he thought would be willing to volunteer for the job. So Andy joined me, and after passing out of the recruit squad, he became my batman. He remained with me for five years and drove me many hundreds of miles in England, the desert, the Middle East and Italy. We became the greatest of friends and he was a tremendous asset to me in keeping in touch with the feelings of the ordinary soldiers. It was largely owing to him that we founded a Toc H group in the regiment. While we were still in England, we visited many Toc H branches in our neighbourhood and had some splendid evenings with them. It was a break for the soldiers from life in the regiment and a boost to the branches who were struggling to keep going in the early days of the war.

Andy created something of a record in the army by joining three different arms of the service. He joined the HAC as Gunner Andrews. When I finally left the regiment to become Senior Chaplain of an armoured division, he moved with me and officially became a tankman and a trooper. When the division was later disbanded and I became Senior Chaplain of an Infantry Division, he moved with me and thus became, officially, an infantryman and a private. In spite of the change of arms, he always insisted in retaining his title of Gunner Andrews. I must admit that his moves were strictly illegal but I had been in the army long enough to know that, if I made a request to higher authority for him to be posted with me, it would have been refused; but if I took him with me, and arrived at my new post, complete with a batman-driver, he would be welcomed with open arms and no further questions would be asked.

Owing to lack of transport in the regiment for the first six months of the war, I had to rely on my glamorous lady driver in her sports car to transport me to my various duties, and Andy remained merely a batman. However, he became an invaluable member of the concert party as well as secretary of the regimental Toc H branch.

For those six months we remained at Elstree, absorbing and training new recruits and sending off small parties to act as guards at a number of so-called 'vulnerable points' in London. One of these was Battersea Bridge and I was invited by the Battery Commander, John Barstow, to visit the troops stationed there. After we had paid our visit, John said, "Let's go and visit my cousin, Peter Fleming; he lives near here and is in bed with flu."

I had known Peter at Oxford and remembered a splendid performance he had given in the OUDS as Iago in *Othello*. He had later made a name for himself as a writer of exciting travel books such as *Brazilian Journey* and *News from Tartary*. We went up to his flat and found him in bed, busily writing. He told us that he was in the middle of a short satirical novel describing how Adolf Hitler had decided that if only he could pay a personal visit to England, he could persuade the country to make peace. He was dropped by parachute into a country village, outside the village hall. By chance a fancy-dress ball was taking place. Hitler walked in and climbed onto the stage and began to make an impassioned speech in German. He was greeted with tremendous applause and given first prize in the fancy-dress competition. Eventually, a quick-witted girl realised who he was and locked him up in the lavatory and telephoned Winston Churchill.

This was as far as Peter had got when we arrived at his bedside. He asked for any suggestions as to how the book could be finished. We left him with the problem unsolved! The book was later published under the title *Flying Visit* with very amusing illustrations, I think by Fougasse. It was strange that it was written before Rudolf Hess actually paid his 'flying visit'. The book ended with Hitler being dropped back into Germany as no one knew what to do with him. It might have been better for Hess if the same thing had happened to him, instead of being subjected to over forty years imprisonment.

The regiment was still doing guard duties at Christmas, and as well as taking services at Elstree, I found myself ministering to small batches of soldiers in such strange places as the tunnel at King's Cross, the waiting room at Holborn Viaduct Station and an elementary school at Hackney. The service in the tunnel was interrupted by smoke fumes every time a train went through.

I completed my duties by taking a Communion Service in the Long Room at Armoury House where a large number of soldiers were billeted. It appears from the records that this is the only time the Long Room has been used for a religious ceremony in the whole history of the regiment. As soon as the service was over the troops sat down to a splendid Christmas dinner.

The regiment moved down to Swanage in the spring of 1940, just before the phoney war came to an end and the Germans invaded Holland, Belgium and France. Swanage is a charming seaside resort and we were billeted in many very comfortable houses, usually occupied by holiday-makers. The weather was very pleasant and spring was followed by one of the loveliest summers I can remember.

Both 'A' and 'B' Batteries were stationed in preparatory schools whose premises had been evacuated. One of them was Forres, which had the added advantage of a school chapel, ideal for our church services. We made great friends with the staff, before they were evacuated, and I grew so fond of the school that later on I sent both my sons there.

My brother, a naval officer, followed my example and, at one time, there were five young Olivers at the school. The last two were nicknamed Quartz and Quin. Sadly, the youngest of these boys was killed in a tragic accident when a mine, sown during the war, exploded while the boys were digging on the beach. Five eleven-year-olds, including my nephew, Jason Oliver, lost their lives.

In many ways Swanage was a delightful change from Elstree. We no longer had the tiresome guard duties in London, and were able to get down to some regimental training, although we were still very short of proper equipment. The accommodation in schools and guest houses was a great improvement on the billets we had in Elstree and altogether our first two months in Swanage were rather like a delightful holiday. The two batteries were settling down and absorbing the recruits who had poured in to replace those who had been selected for officer training.

I was again without transport but was lent a sort of mechanical bicycle by Gerry de Boinville, which enabled me to travel around to do my visiting of hospitals and scattered detachments. Small detachments who were separated from the main body of the regiment often felt rather neglected and left out of things. By getting round and visiting them, I was able to keep them in touch with what was going on, and also find out whether they had any problems in which I could help. Quite often I was asked to take an informal impromptu service even on a weekday. It was useful to remind them that Sunday was not the only day in which God could be worshipped. Unlike the Sunday church parades, these services were of course voluntary.

Altogether the early memories of Swanage are very joyful. The concert party was in great form and took the place of the normal seaside entertainments in the village hall. We played a good deal of cricket and tennis and the war seemed a long way off, with nothing much happening in France, and the unfortunate Norwegian campaign at an end. We were expecting to complete our training and receive our full complement of guns and equipment, then join the First Armoured Division, who were beginning to move over to France.

Suddenly the whole picture changed. The German

Army invaded France, Belgium and Holland and the war was no longer phoney. Alarming reports began to filter over the news, despite a strict censorship, and it became obvious that things were going very badly for the British Army and her allies.

On one lovely summer day we saw out at sea a long stream of ships of all shapes and sizes sailing up the Channel in an easterly direction. Later we realised that they were heading for Dunkirk to take part in the rescue of a large part of our army, and thousands of French soldiers as well.

The news became worse and worse and it was quite clear that the Germans had won a complete victory in France. More and more troops were evacuated from French ports as the Germans gradually established themselves on the coast, and the final disaster for the British was the surrender of the gallant 51st Highland Division at St Valery.

Chapter Two

After Dunkirk

Swanage was no longer a holiday resort. We were suddenly on a war footing and no one doubted that Hitler would attempt an invasion. We still had very little equipment, but a troop of guns was stationed on the hillside above Studland Bay and we maintained a twenty-four hour watch on the coast. I clearly remember getting up at sunrise and doing a two-hour watch before breakfast. I had my leg pulled when I wore my clerical collar, as rumours were rife that German parachutists would very likely be disguised as clergymen.

Towards the end of the summer, moves became frequent. 'A' Battery was sent to the east coast and became, temporarily, the third battery of the 1 RHA now reforming after Dunkirk. I stayed behind with RHQ, and 'B' Battery, and we moved out of Swanage to a most attractive campsite on a hill opposite Corfe Castle. Later on, the two battery regiments gradually sprouted a third battery, the 11th, formed 'E' Battery HAC and 1 RHA took in another regular battery – providing two regiments for the 1st Armoured Division.

Churchill had now formed the Local Defence Volunteers, later called the Home Guard, and we liaised very closely with them. Equipment was still very meagre and there was particularly a shortage of ammunition. The vicar of Corfe kindly offered his church for a Sunday parade and took part in the service with me. During the notices he said to the troops, "There will be a collection but don't worry if you are short of cash, don't bother to put any buttons in the bag, but if you have any spare 303 ammunition, the Corfe Home Guard would be delighted and so would I." Although parsons are supposed to be non-combatants, this was very much the spirit of the country.

On a lovely summer day, towards the end of June, I asked the colonel's permission for a day's leave to visit my mother who was staying with my godmother Evelyn Street, at Cerne Abbas, in their lovely Elizabethan house Upcerne Manor, reputed to have been built by Sir Walter Raleigh. I put my bicycle on a train to Dorchester and then cycled the ten miles through the beautiful Dorset countryside to Cerne Abbas and Upcerne on a lovely summer's day. It was in this idyllic background that we heard the dramatic news that France had signed an armistice with Germany.

Churchill had offered the French joint citizenship with Britain and vowed that he would continue to fight on, but with a few exceptions, the French Cabinet had lost its nerve and Britain was on her own. General de Gaulle was smuggled out of France to form the Free French resistance, but the prospects seemed very black.

As I sat with my mother and Wilfred and Evelyn Street, in their beautiful garden with its private chapel in the background, and heard the dreadful news, it seemed that all that we loved about England and our way of life was coming to an end. The German armies were poised on the coast of France and an invasion seemed inevitable. Although a great part of our army had been evacuated, nearly all their heavy equipment, munitions and armament had been left behind and our chances of resisting the Germans, if they landed in any strength, seemed very slight.

With the threat of invasion now imminent, we were

moved from Dorset to Sussex, as there were several beaches that seemed suitable for invasion. Here 'A' Battery rejoined the 11th.

There was something very exhilarating about living in England in the summer of 1940. Peter Fleming's book *Invasion 1940* gives a wonderful impression of that time. It can be paralleled in history to the threat of the Spanish Armada in 1588 or to the threat of Napoleon in 1805. On both these occasions, we found a leader worthy of our cause. Queen Elizabeth, in her speech at Tilbury in 1588, spoke the same kind of language as Winston Churchill in 1940. The younger Pitt, though not in the same class as an orator, was, like his father, an able politician who united the country behind him. Like Napoleon, in his failure to defeat the Royal Navy, Hitler failed in his attempt to defeat the Royal Air Force. In both cases, in Wellington's words, "It was a damned near thing – the nearest run thing you ever saw in your life."

Churchill's effect on the country's morale was quite dramatic. After so many years in the wilderness, distrusted by all political parties and with very little following in the country, his long-awaited hour had at last struck, so much so, that a German directive in 1942, stated, "The elimination of Churchill must be an essential feature of any attack on British morale."

It is quite clear that Hitler hoped and expected to be able to persuade us to surrender without an invasion. After Dunkirk, he offered an olive branch combined with the threat of massive attack from the air. Without Churchill's defiance, these terms might easily have been accepted.

Peter Fleming suggests that if Hitler had not threatened, but had merely ignored Britain, and proceeded with his other plans for world domination, even Churchill might not have persuaded the country to resist. Suppose, he argues, Hitler had offered to return the 40,000 British prisoners he had captured, how many families would have urged the Government to accept his terms? Hitler never understood the British character. He half admired us as fellow Anglo-Saxons and his advisers suggested that there was a large popular support for National Socialism. Hess's flight to Britain revealed a similar misunderstanding. The threat of invasion, answered by Churchill's defiant oratory, united the country as no olive branch could have done. In spite of that unity and that inspiration, if the Germans had been able to mount an invasion within a few weeks of the fall of France and had landed just a few divisions, our chances of survival would have been slight. We know what the result of a successful invasion would have been: the deportation of all males in the country, aged from seventeen to forty-five, with the exception of potential Quislings, and the seizure of foods and raw materials without any regard to the needs of the remainder of the population. From a military point of view, our chances of successful resistance, in June 1940, were minimal.

In spite of the rescue of a large part of the army, most of its heavy equipment had been abandoned and even the divisions that had escaped, apart from their personal arms, had very few weapons and were completely disorganised. The hastily recruited Local Defence Volunteers (later the Home Guard) were at first issued with little except sporting guns and pitchforks.

Hitler hesitated because he felt quite certain that if we did not agree to make peace at once, some pressure from the German air force would soon bring the country to heel.

Churchill's leadership transformed the situation in a few weeks. In spite of lack of arms, the country became a vast camp. The divisions were pulled together and reorganised. The Home Guard, numbering half a million, recruited every able-bodied man between the ages of seventeen and seventy who could be spared from vital work, producing armaments or food. The air force prepared for the onset of attack from the Luftwaffe.

Women hastily volunteered for any service that could use them and the navy prepared to challenge any attempt on the part of the German army to cross the Channel. Many children were evacuated from danger areas; some even sailed across the Atlantic to Canada and America.

After the initial shock of France's surrender, gradually the feeling in the country changed from bewilderment to determination. We were now on our own, and although our hearts bled for our allies on the continent, now under the heel of the Nazis, we realised we had only ourselves to rely on. We were thrilled by Churchill's words, "We shall never surrender." We loved his sense of humour, his deliberate mispronunciation of the word "Nazis" and his description of Hitler as that "wicked man."

Gradually, we felt that we had a real chance of survival provided we maintained our courage. In the interval between Dunkirk and the start of the air raids, a matter of a few weeks, our leaders gave us confidence that there was now a real plan. If the Germans decided to invade, we would give a good account of ourselves.

Early in July, when Hitler realised we would fight on, the air raids began in real earnest. Their first aim was to destroy our fighter aircraft and several raids were made on all the airfields where the fighters were based. In spite of resistance by our heroic outnumbered airmen, many planes were destroyed on the ground and in the air, and after a couple of months, the fighters were at their last gasp. The cost to the German air force had also been very heavy and, although the British claims were often exaggerated, a heavy toll had been exacted from the enemy, and early in September, still celebrated as the heroic Battle of Britain, Churchill paid his famous tribute, "Never in the course of human history has so much been owed by so many to so few." The Germans switched from day raids to night raids on London and on other industrial cities. These 'terror' raids did a great of damage and caused the loss of thousands of lives, but instead of persuading us to surrender, they stiffened our resolution and our determination "never to surrender."

With the onset of winter, it was quite clear that Hitler had called off the invasion and, although air raids continued, including a ghastly one on Coventry, and a number of so-called 'Baedeker' cities, the main danger of defeat was over, and in 1941, when Germany attacked Russia, we were no longer on our own. Gradually the army and air force were built up again, and with the coming of America into the war, it seemed that prospects of victory were more hopeful.

The effect of war on the attitude of the ordinary soldier, or indeed officer, towards the Christian faith was of course very varied. It shook many of them out of any complacency and made them think of things other than their families and their jobs.

Was there a God? If so, what was He like? How could Christ's teaching about loving all men be equated with a nation at war? I felt it was part of my job to try to answer some of these questions in my preaching at Church parades, and particularly to show the relevance of the Christian faith to the problems they were facing.

Some time ago, I came across a battered notebook containing the notes of many of the sermons I had preached during the first years of the war. Many of them dealt with the basic teaching of the Christian faith: why we believed in God; what difference the coming of Christ into the world made to man's belief in God; what was Christian witness; the power of prayer; eternal life.

But every now and again I felt I must try to explain my attitude as a Christian to this particular war. What were we fighting for? At the time of the threat of invasion in the summer after Dunkirk it was quite clear that we were fighting in defence of our homes and families. To accept the pacifist position was to surrender to an evil tyranny that would be the end of freedom in our country and result in Europe living under the heel of a brutal military despotism for many years to come. As a Christian, one did not hate individual Germans but one did hate the evil of the Nazi doctrine which was completely devilish. We had to rely on God to give us strength and courage to play our part in resisting evil.

It had been a beautiful summer and everything was bone dry. We were soon covered with dust, camping in the woods in the Pallinghurst estate near Loxwood in Sussex. Every time a vehicle went out it raised clouds of dust. At last I had been allotted a car of my own, a small utility. Andy was delighted and soon became a very competent driver and mechanic. He started giving me driving lessons. As I had never possessed a car of my own, having reached the age of thirty-one I was rather slow to learn and poor Andy had some nasty shocks. One day I was at the wheel, and turning a sharp corner, found myself heading towards the public bar of a village pub. To my surprise the car suddenly stopped at the entrance. I looked down and found Andy's hand firmly on the hand brake. "That was a lucky escape," I said. "We had better go in and have a pint."

The problem of keeping clean in the woods was becoming more and more difficult as water was very scarce. At the suggestion of the colonel, Andy and I drove round to a number of houses in the neighbouring villages to enquire whether some of the troops could come and have a bath. We had a wonderful reception and, as far as I can remember, we had no refusals. Indeed, many kind housewives offered to give the soldiers supper as well. This was before rationing, but it shows the wonderful spirit of fellowship that was apparent throughout the whole country, still under the threat of invasion.

Another source of cleanliness was a trip to Christ's Hospital, my old school, to use their swimming baths. We loaded as many as we could into our available three-tonners and thoroughly enjoyed the showers followed by a swim. We returned to the wood of Pallinghurst much refreshed.

By this time the Battle of Britain was raging fiercely and the bombing of London was growing in intensity. We were still under twelve hours notice to move to the coast in the event of invasion. I had a request from my wife's family to go up to Leeds to officiate at the wedding of my sister-in-law. In view of the emergency, I was reluctant to be away from the regiment for too long. After looking up the trains from London, I found I could just about get up and back in one day. The colonel kindly agreed to my going. Andy and I set off at four in the morning. I suggested that he should take me to Morden Station and I could then go on to King's Cross by underground whilst he paid a visit to his family who lived nearby. I asked him to be back at Morden at about 7.30 in the evening to pick me up. I caught the King's Cross express and arrived at Leeds in time for the wedding. It was to be the last time I was to see my in-laws for five years. We had a splendid party. Yorkshire hospitality is famous.

I caught the train back to London and all went well until we arrived at Peterborough. Here the train slowed up and finally came to a halt. While we were wondering what was the cause of the delay, one of my fellow passengers noticed a red glow in the sky, not in the west, where the sun was setting, but in the east. We realised that it must be in the direction of London. It suddenly dawned on us that a massive air raid was in progress. The train went slower and slower and the nearer we were to London, the brighter the sky became. When we finally arrived at King's Cross, the sky was bright red and at the station everything was in a state of confusion and alarm. Although the main raid had been in the docks, bombs had been dropped all over London and many buildings had been hit. It was, by now, nearly nine o'clock and I thought of poor Andy waiting at Morden underground. The underground had stopped running and all traffic appeared to be at a standstill. Everyone was discussing the possibility of this being the prelude to the invasion and I was anxious to get back to the regiment. It was a long walk from King's Cross to Morden!

At various stages I managed to beg a lift, but the air raid alarms kept bringing everything to a standstill and it was after midnight when I finally arrived at Morden station. I had given up all hope of finding Andy. I expected that he would have given me up and gone home to his people. To my surprise and joy, there was the car outside the station with Andy fast asleep at the wheel. It was the first of a number of occasions when he showed me how faithful and reliable he was. We finally got back to camp at about 4 am to find everybody on the alert and ready to move.

It was still being rumoured that the invasion was about to start. I held a short church service at about nine o'clock. By midday the crisis was over and once more, we stood down. In the afternoon I drove over to East Grinstead to christen Howard Bourne's first-born. Howard Bourne was a troop commander and one of the toughest men in the regiment. He was not easy to get to know, but I soon developed a great respect for his staunch qualities and we became great friends. He was killed during the battle of Knightsbridge manning a two-pounder anti-tank gun against an attack by powerful German tanks. His widow married again but still always attends the annual memorial service for the regiment held at the regimental church St Botolph's, Aldersgate on November 11th or the nearest weekday.

At the reception after the service, I passed out and had to be put to bed. The strain of the last forty-eight hours without sleep had finally caught up with me. After a good night's sleep, I woke the next morning completely restored.

By the end of September, it was clear that the invasion had been called off and that the Germans had other plans. The daylight raids had almost ceased but the night bombing of London and other industrial cities continued almost nightly. We now moved further inland and through the winter of 1940–41 were stationed in the neighbourhood of Abinger and Shere in Surrey.

We were now a three-battery regiment ('A', 'B' and 'E'). 'C' and 'D' Batteries were in our second line, the 12th RHA whose third battery was designated 'F'. We did not meet them again until the end of the desert campaign when we landed up at Tunis alongside the 12th, who had landed at Algiers with the First Army.

We soon settled down in our new location, and as usual made many friends in the neighbourhood. I always called on the local vicars to make arrangements to borrow their churches for church parades, which were still compulsory and remained so until the end of the war.

Compulsory church parades were a feature of a chaplain's life in the early days of the war. The army paraded for everything that it regarded as important. It paraded for its pay, it paraded for the doctor and it seemed reasonable to me that it should parade for church. It gave the regiment a feeling of fellowship and community. I felt that it was my responsibility to make the service as interesting and alive as I possibly could. Many years afterward, I found that the same principles applied to a parish church.

I found that very few of the soldiers objected to this kind of service, provided that the "spit and polish" was not too much in evidence and that the NCO's were not too obtrusive. On one or two occasions a man came to see me to say that he had conscientious objections to attending church and I was usually able to see that he was not forced to attend.

One advantage of a church parade was that a man could come to church without being regarded as a 'cissy' by his fellows. Many felt the need for some kind of faith but did not wish to be regarded as "Holy Joes". I remember once in the desert I took a Communion service in pitch darkness. We could not have any light, as enemy aircraft were very busy overhead. One very unexpected man took part and when I said how delighted I was to see him he remarked "It was dark and no one could see I was there." Within many men there is still a feeling they are not good enough to go to church, not realising that no-one is good enough, not even the chaplain, and that church is for sinners rather than saints.

At Abinger, Lionel Meade was the vicar, and as he like myself had been a Toc H chaplain, we very quickly built up a most cordial friendship and I was always warmly welcomed when I called at the vicarage; it became a second home for Andy and myself. Lionel's wife, Gerry, set up a canteen for the troops in the village hall and Andy and I helped her in securing supplies to keep it going.

Another activity was the formation of a regimental dance band to augment the concert party. It began in quite a small way with an accordianist, a saxophonist and a drummer, but gradually grew as various new instrumentalists were posted to the regiment. As no dance band leader appeared, I found myself not only the organiser but also the conductor and even, from time to time, the vocalist. I can still give a fairly reasonable rendering of "I've Got Sixpence," "Mother must I go on Dancing," and other popular dance tunes of the time.

The dance band became a great asset to the regiment and we kept it going until we arrived in Egypt, when the instruments were looted from the troop train on our way from Suez to our first camp at Almaza. Once the dance band was formed, we encountered the problem of acquiring girls for our dances. I scoured the neighbourhood to find suitable candidates, who usually needed ferrying to the dance. I remember my utility truck being stopped by the Military Police, who, on examining the contents, found a dozen young ladies crowded in the back. As I was not wearing my clerical collar, I had to explain that I was the regimental chaplain and that I was carrying 'comforts for the troops' and that the young ladies were not my harem! They let me off with a caution!

I was still getting the usual spate of weddings. Usually the clergy were most co-operative and allowed me to officiate at the service, although one vicar was rather inhospitable and left me a curt note in the vestry which read, "My verger will instruct you in the customs of my church and I expect you to abide by them." On another occasion, the soldier concerned gave me the wrong date and he arrived at the church the day before he had arranged with me. As a result I was alerted by the orderly room that there was a party at church waiting for the chaplain. I dashed out to find Andy and found him washing the car. "Come on Andy," I said. "We're due at Shere church for a wedding." "What," said Andy, "I'm in my Wellington boots." "Don't worry about your Wellington boots, they are waiting at the church." We arrived at the church to find one rather scruffy looking soldier and two girls, one of whom, the bride, was looking distinctly angry. "Is this the whole party?" I asked. "Yes," said the soldier. I explained that he needed another witness to make the service legal. He said that he had just come off a night exercise and had not been able to collect a friend or even to have a bath. At this stage I thought the prospective bride would give up the whole affair so I turned to Andy and said, "Come on Andy, you must be the second witness and give the bride away." "What," said Andy, who had a proper sense of decorum, "in my Wellington boots?" In spite of his Wellington boots, I managed to get the couple safely married and the register signed, and was about to wish them luck and leave the church, when it became obvious that the bridegroom had something on his mind. "What's the matter?" I said. "Off you go." "I haven't anywhere to go," he said. "I've just come off a night exercise." By now the bride was looking really furious, and I must say I rather sympathised with her. However, it was quite clear that unless I took some action, the marriage might end before it had properly begun. "Hold on a minute," I said, "I will ring up the vicar and see if he can suggest something." The vicar, as usual, was most helpful. He was the real old type of village 'squarson' and knew everything that went on in the village. Accommodation was at a premium and I knew that the regiment had requisitioned all the available houses and even the village pubs. "The only thing I can suggest," said the vicar, "is that they come up to the vicarage. They can have my four-poster bed. It has not been used since my dear wife died." So all ended well.

The soldier, who must remain nameless, was subsequently court-martialled for throwing a letter out of the troop train when we were departing for a secret destination, but was later twice decorated for gallantry in action in the desert, and escaping from a prisoner-of-war camp. Another happy ending.

Meanwhile, the regiment was once more getting down to serious training for service overseas. We were now part of the 1st Support Group, a brigade of the First Armoured Division, and we now met for the first time the three cavalry regiments we were going to get to know so well in the desert: the Queen's Bays, the 10th Hussars and The 9th Lancers. Each battery supported its own particular cavalry regiment: 'A', the Bay's 'B', the 10th and 'E', the 9th, an arrangement which lasted the war. We also welcomed our first regular CO, "Baron" Ebbels.

"Baron" Ebbels was the best type of regular officer, and although he only commanded the regiment for two years, he endeared himself to us all and became a permanent member of our reunions after the war. Behind a rather casual appearance, he was completely professional in his approach to the art of gunnery and in battle was utterly fearless. We were very sad when he left us on well-deserved promotion and I was delighted to find him as CRA of the Tenth Armoured Division when I became their senior chaplain at the battle of Alamein.

Although we had several more CO's during the war, the

Baron was always 'the Colonel'. After the war he invariably took the chair at our annual reunions.

After he was widowed, he lived in a flat at the top of Gerry de Boinville's house in Hertfordshire. One day I had a telephone call from his daughter saying that he was very ill and could I go and visit him. As I was getting ready to go, my wife Anne said, "Would it be a good thing to take your Communion Set?" So I did. When I arrived at the house the Colonel was lying in bed apparently unconscious. I asked his daughter whether she would like me to give him communion. She said "I don't think he knows what is going on but I would like it."

We had the service at his bedside. He opened his eyes and received the bread and wine. After the blessing he said, "Thank you Ken, I was hoping that you would do this for me." He died a few days later.

As our previous colonel had frowned on wives coming anywhere near the regiment, it was quite a surprise when the new CO arrived complete with wife, two daughters and three dogs.

At this stage, after Dunkirk, there was a plethora of regular gunners who had lost their batteries. Several were posted to command the three batteries of the HAC and, with regret, we said farewell to Jack Hill our second-in-command and Peter Pettit, who commanded 'B' Battery. They had been members of the regiment for many years and I lost two good friends. These changes were inevitable in times of war and they did bring with them experience of action but caused a good deal of heart-burning in the regiment. We felt that some of the regulars did not always give the territorials, who had given unstinted service for many years in times of peace, a fair deal. This breach was nearly always healed when the test of battle made it very clear who were capable of command. It is interesting to note that during the war in the desert, all three batteries were very ably commanded by original members of the HAC when the regular officers had left on promotion.

We were still in the Abinger and Shere area during Christmas 1940, and many people in the locality were most generous in the hospitality they gave to the troops. One of my pleasant duties was to act as liaison between the regiment and their hosts and I was lucky enough to spend part of Christmas Day with the famous authors, E.M. Forster and Max Beerbohm, both of whom were entertaining soldiers. Our two local vicars, Lionel Meade and Sir Paget Bowman, were always most helpful in suggesting parishioners who would keep open-house for the soldiers. Ralph Vaughan Williams was another generous host.

Our Toc H group arranged to visit several local branches who had managed to keep going. Our visits always seemed to give them a real boost and it gave our new members some idea of what a Toc H branch attempted to achieve in its locality in terms of voluntary social service.

One of the most important officers in a Toc H branch was called the job-master. It was his function to assess the particular needs of the community in which the branch was situated and to allocate to individual members a 'job' for which they were suited. Every member of Toc H was bound by his membership to do a voluntary job of social service. It might be with youth, boys' clubs or scouts, or it might be with the handicapped, the blind or disabled, or with the elderly helping them with gardening which had grown too much for them. In addition to these individual jobs, the branch also took on one or two jobs in which everyone took part together. Every year a Toc H Branch had to submit a job-master's report to enable it to maintain its branch status with the symbol of a Toc H lamp.

For the musically minded soldiers, (classical, not pop) I was able to form a group, and we received a very pleasant invitation from a firm that had been evacuated from

London to Dorking, to a musical tea-party on a Sunday afternoon, in the firm's office. This became a regular Sunday feature and when rumours of the splendid teas began to circulate around the regiment, the number of soldiers who appreciated classical music, swelled appreciably and I had no trouble in gathering a good number of applicants.

With all these activities, I found plenty to occupy my time, and in addition I was often used by the orderly room as a trouble-shooter when the military clashed with the civilian world. Our regimental headquarters was situated in a large country house in Abinger Hammer. Part of it was still occupied by a formidable dowager who was apt to complain about various activities of both officers and men. The colonel was terrified of her and when things came to a head he used to send me in to pacify her. "Padres are used to dealing with difficult women," he said. "She will respect your cloth." Strangely enough, she did.

On another occasion, the wife of one of the soldiers was had up in court on the charge of stealing another girl's handbag at a dance. The soldier went to the adjutant in great distress. The result was that I was asked to accompany him to the magistrates' court. When the case came up, the counsel for the defence could not say very much on behalf of his client, so he said to the Bench, "The soldier's chaplain is in court," and to my horror, I found myself called upon to address the court. I did the best I could, saying that this gallant young man had volunteered to serve his country and what a splendid fellow he was. The Chairman of the Bench cut me short and remarked, "That's all very well, padre, but we are not trying the man, but his wife." I sat down feeling rather foolish. However, the girl got off with a warning, so perhaps I did some good.

On another occasion, a young soldier had been spending his honeymoon at a local hotel and had not enough money to pay the bill. Not unnaturally, the manager impounded all their luggage. Once more I was sent off to see what I could do. The hotel was some way away and my car was in dock. I went down to see the transport officer to enquire whether he could lend me a vehicle. At first he said he had nothing available and then, looking up, he saw an armoured car with its engine starting up. "You can take that if you like, padre. It has to do a road test." So I jumped in beside the driver and set off for the hotel. When I saw the manager in his office, at first he was not very helpful. Suddenly his expression changed and I saw he was looking out of the window. "All right," he said, "You can take the luggage with you." Surprised at this sudden change, I turned around and looked out of the window. To my astonishment, the gun from the armoured car was pointing straight through the window at the manager as the driver backed the car. I wondered whether he thought that he was being attacked, but I collected the luggage and departed before he changed his mind.

From time to time, I was asked to run the officers' mess but I was not much of a success. My crowning disaster occurred when we were entertaining the colonel of the Saskatchewan Light Infantry. The Canadian division were doing an exercise with us, and to the horror of our colonel, we ran out of the Canadian's favourite drink, scotch on the rocks. I was rapidly replaced as mess secretary!

The regimental training was accelerating and I remember one exercise when we were out at night in particularly atrocious weather. Eventually, I was able to find a country pub where we set up regimental headquarters and managed to put our sleeping bags in the saloon bar and get a few hours sleep in comparative comfort.

In the early summer of 1941, we moved to Chilton Foliat, near Hungerford, which was to be our last station before going abroad. We were stationed in Chilton Park in pleasant hutted accommodation. The officers' mess was in Chilton Lodge, a very attractive Georgian house belonging to Lady Ward. She kindly allowed us to use the dining room and billiard room while she occupied the rest of the house. We all slept in the huts, as did the soldiers. Lady Ward was another formidable dowager and, as in previous situations, the colonel used me as liaison officer when trouble occurred. Fortunately, our relationships, on the whole, were very friendly. We thoroughly enjoyed the use of her excellent tennis court. I teamed up with the doctor, Dudley Yarrow, my usual partner, and we managed to win the regimental doubles championship.

Chilton Foliat was a most attractive village and, as in our previous billets, the people living there went out of their way to make us welcome. A canteen was set up in the church hall and most of the soldiers found some house where they were made very much at home.

The vicar, Walter Pelham, like his counterpart at Shere, was an old-fashioned parson, very much the father of the village. He and his family became great friends and could not do enough to make the regiment feel at home. The river Kennet ran through the village and the vicarage garden. We arrived during the time of the mayfly and Mrs Pelham, an enthusiastic fisherwoman, was kind enough to allow several other keen fishermen to angle in the vicarage glebe.

Another big house in the neighbourhood was the Elizabethan manor of Littlecote, owned by the Wills family. They allowed us to borrow their cricket ground and we managed to play a number of the local village teams.

The village church is an architectural gem and Walter Pelham gave us 'carte blanche' for our Sunday church parades. After the war I was offered the job of vicar of Chilton Foliat, but by that time, I had decided to stay on in the army.

Hungerford was only a couple of miles away and we

soon made contact with many people there. They possessed a splendid Town Hall which I found very useful for all kinds of entertainments for the troops. The dance band especially, came into its own and we organised regular Saturday night dances. By now the band had become quite accomplished, although it still lacked a proper leader or conductor. So once more I found myself 'the leader of the band' and also the main crooner, much to the amusement of the locals, who did not expect to see an army chaplain in such a role!

The dances were a great success and formed a most useful link between the younger soldiers and the local families. We also made quite a good sum of money for the regimental funds, which came in very useful for buying comforts for the troops, which could not be purchased through regular channels. The funds also provided a certain influence with the second-in-command.

The army issued all chaplains with a number of small prayer-books which contained Morning and Evening Prayer, the service of Holy Communion and a number of the better known hymns from *Hymns Ancient and Modern*. I found these rather inadequate, as there were a number of more recent hymns which would be most suitable for my services. I approached the second-in-command, Tishy Benson, as to the possibility of having an additional hymnbook printed which would contain some more rousing hymns. Tishy said that he did not consider it a legitimate charge on the regimental funds. "I don't think it is really necessary, Padre."

However, when I pointed out the large sums of money I had produced for the regimental funds from the dances I had organised in the local town hall, he agreed rather grudgingly. We had them printed and they proved a great asset to the services, especially on board ship and in the desert.

One night, I was in one of the local pubs when a man came up to me and asked if I could help him. His son was in trouble with the regimental police over the possession of some firearms. I cannot quite remember the details, but I managed to straighten the matter out. The boy was quite innocent of any offence. As a result, to my embarrassment, I was always given free drinks whenever I went into the pub. When the regiment left, the grateful father gave me a handsome donation towards the regimental funds.

It became clear that we were soon to be sent abroad. Rumours abounded as to where it would be. Wavell's victories in the desert, largely organised by General O'Connor, an old member of the regiment, made the Middle East the most popular bet. Security was very tight and gossip about our destination was frowned on by authority.

Royal visits heightened the tension. George VI and Queen Elizabeth spent a day with us and had tea in the officers' mess. After tea, the officers were photographed with their Majesties, the king being our Captain-General. The photograph with the full list of all the officers, many of whom, alas, were killed in action and never returned home is reproduced in this book. We were visited as well by the Duke of Gloucester, also a member of the regiment. The Duke was a man of few words and very shy. He walked solemnly around the room and shook hands with all the officers, signed the visitors' book and retired without saying a word, although outside, when saying goodbye to the colonel, he managed to say, "Good luck!"

On the social side, a final spate of marriages took place, amongst them, Roger Croxton and Arthur Green's. Roger Croxton and Arthur Green were two of the staunchest members of the regiment. Roger formed 'E' Battery and although he was once replaced by a regular major, the latter was posted away just before we went abroad and Roger was reappointed to command the battery. He was a most conscientious and gallant soldier. He was badly wounded at Knightsbridge, but had proved himself an inspiring leader during all the difficulties of

Jock Columns and the testing battle of Knightsbridge.

Arthur Green became adjutant just before we went abroad and was always a tremendous help to me. He was a very keen churchman and I could always rely on his advice, judgement and assistance. Both he and Roger remained great friends and are still supporters of our reunions forty years after.

Arthur was captured during a particularly unpleasant night action outside Mersa Matruh. I heard afterwards that his administrative abilities were a great asset in his prison camp. He always found an outlet for his great energy and ability whatever the circumstances and he was less affected by three years in a prisoner-of-war camp than almost anyone I ever knew.

These weddings gave us a good excuse to go to London and have a last taste of the delights of the city.

As a grand finale, Lady Ward very kindly allowed us to have a farewell ball in her house. The regimental dance band, still led by the chaplain, were dressed in a magnificent uniform hired from Archie Nathan, a member of the Regiment, and last used in Noel Coward's "Bitter Sweet" for his Hungarian Hussars. Bright blue with silver facings, they looked magnificent and the evening was a wonderful climax to our last days in England. We also ran a final dance for the soldiers in the Hungerford Town Hall, when they were able to say farewell to their girlfriends.

A few days later we marched at night to Hungerford station and embarked for an unknown destination. Our new second-in-command, a regular soldier, arranged for the officers' kit to be taken to the station, two miles away, by lorry, but as all the troops were laden with their heavy kitbags for the night march, the officers decided to carry their own as they marched alongside the men. A typical HAC gesture.

Chapter Three

Into Battle

After a tedious train journey, we finally reached the docks at Liverpool and embarked on His Majesty's Troopship *Samaria.* She sat in the dock for several days and then had a number of false starts, but we finally set sail for an unknown destination.

An amusing incident happened during that time. Captain Howard Bourne had been sent ashore on some last-minute errand and arrived back at the docks to see the ship leaving her berth, apparently setting off on her voyage. However, determined not to be left behind, he badgered the dock officers to lend him a tug to catch the ship up. In frantic haste he set off, only to see the ship calmly mooring again only a hundred yards from the shore. He was loudly cheered as he clambered up the ship's side.

It was my first journey out of England and I always had the reputation in the family of being a poor sailor. Both my brothers were in the Royal Navy and claimed that I had been seasick when setting out for a short trip in a rowing boat at Worthing. However, after one brief spell in my cabin when we first encountered the Atlantic rollers, I thoroughly enjoyed our ten weeks' spell in the troopship and found that my sea legs were quite steady. Unfortunately, my brief spell of seasickness coincided with a Sunday church parade, which I was unable to take.

The OC Troops, a retired colonel, volunteered to deputise for me. He rather upset his congregation by beginning his sermon with the words, "I am not a religious man!" Actually, he was a splendid Christian and was simply being rather modest and humble.

The most upsetting feature of our voyage was the vast discrepancy in accommodation between the officers and the other ranks. The officers had the typical first-class accommodation of a P & O luxury liner though rather more than one to a cabin. I shared a cabin with three other officers: Ron Norwood, the REME officer, Teddy Henchman, the signals officer, and Quentin Drage, a young subaltern. Ron Norwood became one of my greatest friends and a member of the group that still meets regularly over forty years later.

Quentin Drage was a most charming and talented young man who eventually won the MC and became adjutant of the regiment. He survived the desert campaign but was killed in almost the last battle that the regiment took part in, the Gothic Line in Northern Italy. Many years afterwards, I was visiting Hatfield House and the lovely church at Old Hatfield, and I came across a memorial to Quentin, placed in the church by his family. He was one of the many gallant young men whose death was a sad loss to the country. He would have had a splendid career had he survived the war.

My third companion, Teddy Henchman, was a very cheerful soul. He left the regiment on promotion during the early days of the desert but survived the war.

Both Teddy and Quentin were over six feet tall and the cabin rather crowded. Ron and I, being the two seniors, had the privilege of lying in bed while the others dressed and shaved and left a clear space for us to do the same.

We fed like fighting cocks and drink was cheap and plentiful. The other ranks were not so fortunate and were stowed away in the bowels of the ship, sleeping in hammocks or on the deck. Their food also was pretty unpalatable and there was terrible overcrowding everywhere. Fortunately, we had the whole regiment together and the relationship between the officers and men was very close so we all did our best to make the men's life as bearable as possible. We were fewer than half of the total number on board and many of the other soldiers had no officers to take an interest in their welfare. This was particularly true of a large draft of men of the Royal Air Force. Their officers had no real connection with them as they were simply drafts, and appeared to take no interest in the other ranks. The regimental tradition was a great asset to the army, and the officers always made sure that the men were comfortable and properly fed before they had their own meals.

We were off on a very great adventure; we had been together for two years and apart from experiencing some air raids had not been tested in battle.

Apart from two regular majors in Jeff Linton and Tishy Benson, and our CO Baron Ebbels, and two regular captains, Brian McLaren and Robin Dunn, the remainder of the other officers were nearly all HAC members. The subalterns were a splendid crowd. The HAC had provided hundreds of commissions in the Royal Artillery and we had been able to demand a very high standard amongst those who wished to return to us. I have never met a finer band of young twenty-year olds.

The NCO's contained a number of old and tried HAC members who had decided not to apply for a commission, possibly because they felt they were too old, but more probably out of loyalty to the regiment, combined with a sprinkling of regulars.

The other ranks were almost all volunteers, many of whom had joined us on the outbreak of war. We had been able to weed out a few who we thought would not stand the strain of action and in the event we had very few failures.

The pride of belonging to the oldest military body in

England was to prove a tremendous asset in battle. I consider myself most fortunate that I had been allowed to remain with them for two years. Very few chaplains had been so lucky.

Our personal relationship with God was not spoilt by our involvement in a war to defend all that we held dear in our country. In the faith of Jesus Christ, everyone was given the opportunity of an unbreakable link with Our Father, God. His presence never left us. As the old Civil War commander general, Sir Jacob Astley, once prayed before going into battle: "Oh God I may forget you, do not forget me."

The other constant theme was the love of those we had left behind. I remembered a sermon on "God Bless you" in which I tried to explain what the phrase meant and how the prayers of our loved ones brought them close to us in spirit, though far away from them in body.

As far as I can remember, we did not know exactly where we were going although the issue of khaki drill made it apparent that we were going East, but it might be either the Far East or the Middle East. This provided a great feeling of curiosity and expectancy. I discovered a text from Genesis: "Abraham went forth, not knowing whither he was going."

For a chaplain, the long voyage was an ideal opportunity of really getting to know all ranks. I tried never to forget the slogan over Tubby Clayton's room in the Old House at Poperinghe, "All rank abandon ye who enter here." To a chaplain, a private is just as important as a general and, although the chaplain had the privilege of officer status, he had to make sure that he approached all ranks in exactly the same way. My time in Toc H was a marvellous training for my years in the army and it was vital that I spent as much time below decks with the troops as I did with the officers in their luxurious first-class accommodation.

I still have the ship's orders appointing me Ship's

Entertainment Officer. I had managed to bring the dance band's instruments on board and this proved a great asset in organising concerts and other musical entertainments.

We held regular Toc H meetings and arranged as many talks and discussions as we could, as life was very boring for those below decks. The weather, when we set off, was cold and we soon encountered Atlantic gales.

We were part of one of the largest convoys ever to leave the country, and we were escorted by a most impressive array of naval ships: a number of destroyers, an aircraft carrier and the battle cruiser, HMS *Devonshire*. The convoy was a most impressive sight, with the troopships, tankers and other vessels surrounded by the ships of the Royal Navy. Most of the mornings were taken up with boat-deck drill, which was not very popular and rather monotonous. However, when we were two days out, we spotted a German plane and we realised the necessity of the drill and tackled it with considerably more enthusiasm. We expected a bombing raid to follow the spotter plane and the prospect of being in an open boat in the bleak and inhospitable Atlantic Ocean was not an encouraging one. There were also a number of submarine scares, and for the first few days, alarms were fairly frequent. In the event, we were extremely fortunate, and after ten weeks at sea, we arrived at Port Tewfik at the southern end of the Suez Canal, unscathed.

In order to avoid enemy aircraft and submarines, we sailed as though we were heading for America, and as we were going South we soon came into warmer weather. We found our sea legs and the voyage became much more pleasant. The regiment began serious training, although we did not know whether we were going to Egypt, India or the Far East.

Our first port of call was Freetown. Unfortunately, the climate was considered rather unhealthy and we were not allowed on shore, which was a great disappointment after fourteen days at sea. We were besieged by locals in their tiny boats, trying to persuade us to buy very tempting looking fresh fruit. We were forbidden to buy anything from them owing to the danger of contamination. The native boys then begged us to throw coins into the sea so that they could exhibit their prowess in diving for them. Eventually, even this palled, and we were left sweltering in the heat. It was probably a good preparation for the climate that we would encounter later on, but in a ship built for the Atlantic, at anchor near the shore, it was really oppressive. There was no relief at night and most of us slept on deck. Even now, I can still remember the feeling of even one's ears being full of perspiration.

One of the objects of calling at the port was to take on fresh water but, owing to some hitch in the proceedings, our ship had difficulty in obtaining the full amount. This meant that, not only were we the last ship to leave, but also that there was an acute shortage of fresh water before we reached our next port of call. We did not pick up the convoy for another forty-eight hours and, in the meantime, there was another submarine scare. Altogether our memories of Freetown were not very happy.

Our next port of call was Durban and here we had a wonderful reception from the local inhabitants. As we steamed into the harbour, there was a line of cars stretching as far as the eye could see, waiting to greet us. Bands were playing, flags flying, a woman dressed in white singing over a loud speaker and crowds of people cheering and waving. As we stepped off the ship's gangway, the cars drove up and offered to take us to their homes for a meal and a drive around the town and its environs. Although there were many thousands of troops in the convoy, none went without some kind of most generous hospitality.

The HAC were particularly fortunate. A former member of the regiment was one of the most prominent and wealthy citizens of Durban and he had been waiting for the arrival of his beloved regiment. He had a beautiful house on the outskirts of the town and he entertained us most royally. His attractive daughters and their girlfriends soon made friends with the younger officers. In the garden there were a swimming pool and tennis court and the few days we spent in Durban passed all too quickly.

When they heard we had a regimental dance band, they hastily arranged a magnificent ball. It was the swan-song of our band as our instruments were looted on the train journey from Suez to the Delta, a few weeks later. It was also my last appearance as crooner and dance band leader! It was a memorable ending to many enjoyable evenings with the regimental dance band.

Durban is a most attractive city with beautiful beaches and picturesque countryside within easy reach. One day, some of us were taken for a drive to the Valley of a Thousand Hills. Here we caught a glimpse of the life of the indigenous people in South Africa and, in spite of the segregation between black and white, the atmosphere appeared very friendly and pleasant.

When the time came to say farewell to Durban and our generous hosts, Mr James sent down to the ship a vast amount of fruit, delicacies, sweets and cigarettes, for the benefit of the soldiers. Some of these unfortunately suffered the same fate as the band's instruments on the train in Egypt, but much of it was a welcome addition to our camp diet when we finally arrived at Amyria.

As we turned north to sail up the Red Sea, we said farewell to the battle cruiser, *Repulse*, which had accompanied us in our convoy. We lined the decks and gave her a salute as she sailed through the convoy. She was a magnificent sight and seemed to embody all the strength and grace of the Royal Navy. Alas, she sailed to the Far East and was sunk, with the *Prince of Wales*, in a Japanese air attack a few weeks later, much to our sorrow. This sinking was one of the reasons for the loss of Singapore.

While we were at sea, we also heard of the sinking of the *Ark Royal.* I had made particular friends with the ship's wireless officers; we met regularly in their cabin for pre-lunch drinks, at what became known as the 'Dirty Bottoms Club' because our battle dress, grimy from the heat of the day, soiled their immaculate white covers. They knew that I had both my brothers in the *Ark Royal* and gave me the news before it was generally released. It was some time before the details of casualties were announced and I spent an anxious forty-eight hours wondering whether they were safe. I also felt for my mother, who had her three sons all at sea at the same time. In the event, both my brothers were saved, with the majority of the ship's crew. My elder brother was the ship's chief engineer and he was awarded the OBE for his share in keeping the ship afloat for twenty-four hours, thus enabling the greater part of the crew to be taken off. He had to scramble down the ship's side and suffered a wound on his leg which still plays up from time to time. My younger brother, who was only twenty-two, was working with him and was mentioned in despatches. I believe they were the only two members of the crew who were decorated in this action.

We went ashore at Aden, where we visited the war memorial to members of the regiment who were killed in the First World War.

Following a visit to Port Sudan, we arrived at Port Tewfik after a ten-week voyage. It was with great relief that we finally said farewell to His Majesty's Troopship *Samaria.* Afterwards, we remembered her with affection and we have a memento of the ship at Armoury House. In 1983 we had a reunion of those who sailed on her forty-two years ago and remembered those of our comrades who failed to return home.

We arrived at Suez early in December, and to our amazement, were ordered to wear battledress. Sailing up the Red Sea, we had been so hot that we expected to be in khaki drill in Egypt but, in fact, cold winds were the order of the day with most unpleasant sandstorms constantly springing up. We were glad of battledress and greatcoats. We were only dissuaded from wearing 'caps-comforter' by the sergeant major's command, "Take that clown's hat off."

Our first camp, Amyria was on the outskirts of the desert. It was a typical desert camp about fifteen miles out of Alexandria; apart from a few native shanties and one or two hutted buildings it was entirely composed of tents.

As a reinforcement camp, it acted as a staging post between the ports and the desert, giving us a good preview of what the desert would be like. Dusty and uncared for, it had little to commend it, and as soon as our duties were over we made hotfoot for the delights of Alexandria which possessed all the amenities the troops required. We realised it was probably our last chance for some time of tasting the delights of civilisation. I was delighted to find a Toc H Services Club in Alexandria, run by a very friendly man called Williams. He told us we could come and stay there when we had any leave. There was also a Fleet Club for sailors, run by another Toc H man called Dickie Dines, and a naval chaplain, Alan Spender. When I arrived to call on them, there was a rather formidable notice which said "Out of bounds to soldiers." Apparently, there had been a number of fights between soldiers and sailors after too many drinks. However, when I explained how well behaved the HAC were and that we had a branch of Toc H in the regiment, Dickie added at the bottom of the notice, "Except to members of the HAC." As a result, we had several splendid evenings at the club.

By now the regiment was equipped with the necessary guns and vehicles and we were ready to follow up the victorious Desert Army which had defeated Rommel after a hard fought battle, and relieved Tobruk. Rommel had retreated beyond Benghazi, and was expected to stand on a narrow front at El Agheila.

Officers of the regiment photographed with George VI and Queen Elizabeth before leaving for overseas in 1941

(*above*) At Bir el Gubi, May 1942

(*above right*) A Service in the desert, 1943

(*right*) The Toc H Canteen

(*below*) Soldiers' graves in the Middle East

(*above*) Andy and the Padre

(*left*) Monty with Kenneth Oliver at the Royal Army Chaplains' Depot., Bagshot Park for the dedication of the Memorial Chapel, 1951

(*below*) With Bishop Bardsley at a Christian Leadership Course in Germany

Receiving the CBE at Buckingham Palace in 1960, accompanied by my sister and my aunt

We set off with the three armoured regiments that we expected to support in the battle. 'A' Battery, with the Queen's Bays, 'B' with the 10th Hussars and 'E' with the 9th Lancers. I expected to be with 'B' and the 10th Hussars, as both the other armoured regiments had C of E chaplains and the 10th, a Roman Catholic, who would be attached to the Field Ambulance during the battle.

I was hoping to have a vehicle of my own, as I needed to be able to visit the various parts of the regiment who were split up over the whole divisional area. However, in the event no vehicle was available. Later, I gathered my truck had been taken by an extra staff officer at Brigade Headquarters. I therefore had to do the first part of the journey on a three-ton truck travelling with six other soldiers including, of course, Andy, and all our kit and other regimental supplies.

On December 12th, we set off on the first lap of our journey to Mersa Matruh, a distance of a hundred and eighty miles. An armoured brigade spread out over the desert was a most impressive and exhilarating sight. Owing to the threat of attack from the air, each vehicle had to be fifty yards away from its neighbour and as the brigade must have had well over one thousand vehicles, we covered a considerable amount of ground.

The tanks were Crusaders and the American Honeys. The Crusaders especially, with their sleek contours, looked quite splendid as they drove in lines at about twenty miles an hour. It was only later that we realised their inadequacy in armour and fire-power when facing formidable German Mark III's and IV's with their thicker armour and more powerful guns. They were also too delicate to stand up to the tough going in the desert.

There were basically three types of 'going'. The first was beautifully smooth and flat, when you could drive at almost any speed in the greatest comfort. The second was pitted with boulders and stones of every type which the vehicles bucketed over at about five miles an hour. The first time we encountered this type, our driver was horrified and said, "If we get much of this, the poor truck will break its back." Before we had finished we had plenty of experience of that. The third type was even worse: soft sand in which the vehicles soon got bogged down, sometimes right up to the axle. We then had to dig out with spades and sand channels which were placed under the wheels. As the drivers became more experienced, they learned to spot the soft sand and attempt to avoid it, or if this was impossible, to stop before we dug in too deeply, and put sand channels under the wheels. This was a very slow and laborious process and became rather hair-raising when we knew the German tanks or armoured cars were not far behind.

We soon mastered our daily routine. Starting early in the morning, having washed and shaved and had breakfast, we drove until about midday when, if we were lucky, we stopped for some food and a quick brew-up of strong sweet tea. At about 17.00 hours we moved into a close laager for the night and cooked our main meal.

We cooked on a vehicle basis, each small team taking care of itself. We were issued with a week's ration of food and water. As we were used to having our meals cooked by regimental cooks on a battery basis, it took a little time to get used to cooking in small parties for ourselves. Our fire was usually made up of petrol and sand, very wasteful but the only way, unless we happened to stop near some camel thorn. We constructed home-made ovens, frying pans and kettles, out of empty petrol cans. These were made of aluminium and known as 'flimsies'. They were so flimsy that, after a few miles of hard going in the desert, they soon sprang leaks and the amount of petrol wasted was quite perturbing. It was nearly a year later when we finally copied the Germans and produced the much stouter and reliable 'Jerry Can'. By this time, many thousands of gallons of precious petrol had been wasted. However, the flimsies had proved very useful in the construction of cooking utensils after they had been emptied of petrol. The petrol fumes dispersed after a few days use!

Rations were very scarce and water was limited to half a gallon per man, per day, for all purposes, including keeping the radiators topped up. This meant that one could only use a mugful for washing and shaving, as three pints were required for brewing up. The food was mainly bully beef and biscuits with a little tinned bacon and some margarine. We became quite expert in devising variations of this limited diet. For our first six weeks we lived on this with very little addition, even on Christmas day. For breakfast, we had fried bully, biscuits and tea, for lunch, cold bully, biscuits and tea and in the evening, stewed bully, perhaps with a cube of Oxo, biscuits and tea! In spite of this rather monotonous menu, we kept remarkably fit and regular in our habits. There were, of course, no lavatories, we just walked out into the desert with a spade!

At night, we slept around the three tonner. Officers had a camp bed and everyone was issued with a small bivouac tent. However, when we were on the move, we seldom bothered to pitch our bivvy tents, a difficult job in a wind, and unless it was raining, we slept out in the open.

The weather at this time of year was pretty cold, often with a most unpleasant wind, from which there was very little protection, as all we could see was miles and miles of flattish desert with not a tree in sight.

Travelling on a three-ton truck with six other soldiers was a rather frustrating experience but at least I got to know my fellow travellers very well and had a very clear view of how the ordinary soldier felt and thought. We lived cheek by jowl and I took my fair share of all the necessary duties, especially in the preparation of meals.

While we were travelling, it was often impossible to take any services during daylight hours. On Sundays, I took the opportunity in the evening, when we came into our close laager and had consumed our evening meal, of having a few simple prayers or possibly a hymn we all knew by heart, usually either "Abide With Me," or "The King of Love my Shepherd is," or "There is a green hill far away."

We continued in this fashion for nearly four hundred miles, passing Mersa Matruh and then the Egyptian-Libyan frontier. This was at the top of a very formidable escarpment which we climbed through a track known as Halfaya Pass, naturally nicknamed 'Hell-fire' by the soldiers. It was here that we heard our first sounds of battle as the guns of 30 Corps had surrounded the German garrison in the fortress on the coast.

We crossed the ravine in a blinding sandstorm in which it was difficult to keep in touch with our column. In another day or two we reached Tobruk which, in the distance, was a delightful looking fort, but on closer inspection, much damaged by the siege with the harbour still full of wrecks.

Outside Tobruk, we were stationary for a few days and took the opportunity of cleaning ourselves up and washing clothes. Water was still scarce, washing arrangements were pretty primitive, and it was still bitterly cold. It was nearly cold enough to freeze the water. I remember Christmas Day very vividly as I managed to get around the batteries with the Communion set, taking services wherever we could find some shelter from the bitter wind.

I always found Communion in the desert particularly moving. I usually recced a site the day before, preferably in a sheltered waadi. The altar was either a rock or the back of a truck. A small cross and a white linen cloth (often difficult to keep clean) were the only ornaments. My Communion set, a simple chalice and paten and some battered army prayerbooks, our sole equipment. The elements usually consisted of army biscuits and rough local wine, and water was very scarce. After our first brush with the enemy I lost my cassock and surplice; a stole over my shirt and shorts was my only vestment. I suppose it was the stark simplicity that made the service so moving. The congregation, usually quite small, stood around in a semi-circle and knelt to receive. At these moments God seemed even closer than in a building and the war seemed a long way off.

Christmas was just another day – cold and bleak.

Various attempts were made to acquire some local vino to help the party spirit, but it was our first Christmas away from home and we missed our families dreadfully. Many of the men wrote long letters home, and as we officers censored them, we noticed a special depth of love and warmth.

I cannot remember that we ever exchanged presents. We had nothing to give, but I think we were less demanding as we shared our meagre rations.

Owing to the failure of our Christmas fare to arrive in time, our Christmas Dinner was the usual bully beef and biscuits. We were incensed when we heard over the wireless that "the troops in the desert were enjoying tinned turkey and Christmas pudding." Ours arrived a few days later, as we were far away from any NAAFI dumps and the quartermaster's column had many miles of desert to travel.

Early in January we were separated from our armoured regiments and split up into what were known as 'Jock Columns'. These were composed of a battery of guns and a company of mechanised infantry. We were supported by the 2nd Battalion of the Rifle Brigade. The idea was to keep in touch with the enemy who had retreated behind the El Agheila line. He was supposed to be short of tanks. The columns were to get near enough to fire at any possible targets, but to retreat if the German tanks came out to attack us, as our tanks were about one hundred miles behind us, many of the Crusaders having broken down owing to the heavy going.

Our guns were towed by rather clumsy vehicles known as 'quads'. If we were operating in soft sand, it was very easy for the guns and their quads to get bogged down in the sand. One of the rather strange things about desert warfare was that neither side wanted the desert and if one was outnumbered and outgunned, there was no point in standing to fight. One retired to fight again another day.

The other factor was that 'soft-skinned' vehicles could not take on tanks or armoured cars. As all vehicles in the Jock Columns were soft-skinned, it meant that when the tanks appeared, the only sensible thing to do was to make oneself scarce.

This explains a good deal of what happened to us during our three-months' experience of Jock Columns. After a day or two, while we became accustomed to this particular type of operation, we suddenly became involved in one of Rommel's unexpected forays. The truck on which I was travelling was attached to 'James Column' commanded by Lt Col Jimmy Bosvile, CO of the Rifle Brigade, and included 'B' Battery with whom I usually found myself in battle. My truck was ordered to find another vehicle that had broken down, and Andy and I were deposited in the desert to write some letters. We heard some firing that seemed to be getting nearer and suddenly some vehicles from the column came driving past us, heading east and shouting out, "Come on, Rommel's tanks are just behind!" We scrambled onto one of the vehicles and drove some miles in an easterly direction and gathered that the guns had been engaged with a large number of German tanks and had suffered several casualties. We learned later that the Germans had managed to get reinforcements for their tanks unbeknown to our intelligence. Rommel had decided to make a reconnaisance in force to test our strength. When he found that there were no tanks in our columns, he drove through them and advanced a hundred miles before encountering the tanks of the 2nd Armoured Brigade.

Meanwhile, the scattered elements of the Jock Columns had to get back to Tobruk as best they could. In fact, we spent nearly a week behind Rommel's lines. The vehicle that Andy and I had been travelling on was captured by the Germans with all our kit, except my Communion set, which was never supposed to leave my side. In my kit was my school-leaving Bible, which I had been given when I left Christ's Hospital. I was very upset at losing it. It turned up again in a remarkable way some years later when I was supervising the establishment of chaplaincy services in a large prison camp full of Germans captured at the end of the campaign.

One of the problems in the desert was to make sure we did not run out of petrol. As the scattered vehicles of the Jock Columns made their way back to safety, it must be remembered, that apart from the coast road, there were no proper roads, only tracks, and we had to find our way by compass bearings. Most of the trucks had sun compasses, as ordinary compasses were not easy to operate in a moving vehicle. After we had driven a number of miles we were fortunate enough to encounter some petrol trucks, just as our supplies were getting rather low. As we clustered around the petrol truck, we were suddenly attacked by dive-bombing Stukas, supported by slower moving Italian CR42's. As instructed, we ran as far from our trucks as we could and lay on the ground trying to bury ourselves in the sand. The noise of the dive-bombers was horrifying and several vehicles, including the petrol truck, were hit and set ablaze. After the Stukas, came the CR42's flying very low and very slowly, machine-gunning the area around the trucks. It was our first experience of this type of attack and it was quite terrifying. But in spite of the noise and the columns of dust and smoke, no one was injured. Later on, in similar attacks, we realised that if we kept away from our truck and lay low, the chances of being hit were fairly remote but the first two or three times we experienced this sort of attack, it was quite a test of morale.

It was approaching dusk as we closed in for our night

laager. We had a cold supper of the usual bully beef and biscuits but could not have our usual brew-up of tea, or anything hot, as we did not wish to expose our position, for we suspected the Germans might be near.

It was here that I conducted my first burial, of a soldier killed in another column. We wrapped the body in a blanket and dug a grave in the sand. We marked the position with a cross but we were in an isolated part of the desert and had not much hope of its ever being found. I took as accurate a map reference as I could and despatched it to Rear Divisional HQ, with a spare identity disc and what personal possessions the soldier had on him. Some years later, when I was visiting the War Cemetery in Bengazhi, I found the grave of the soldier marked there. The War Graves Commission had found our hastily constructed grave and reburied the soldier in the main cemetery. This is only one example of the magnificent work done by the Commission.

With our duties completed, we were about to settle down for the night, when we heard the sound of vehicles approaching. It was a German convoy, and they too settled down for the night, far too close for comfort. We were warned to keep silent and to be ready for a quick getaway at 4 am the next morning. As we tried to get some sleep, we saw the coloured rockets that the Germans used to direct their supply convoys, usually a sinister green colour. It was rather an odd situation during a mobile battle, that enemy laagers often settled down for the night within sound of each other. We could distinguish friend from foe by the rockets the enemy sent up. Our laagers had no such signal. Unless a definite attack was ordered, no one disturbed a night laager, and the rockets often gave us a clear idea where danger lay when we were retreating at night.

We had hardly any sleep that night and at 4 am we quietly packed up our sleeping bags and prepared for a quick getaway. Andy and I were travelling in a fifteen-hundredweight truck with Mike Page and four other soldiers. No sooner had we started the engine up and made a start, we found ourselves bogged down in soft sand. Furiously, we started to dig ourselves out but the wheels were deeply embedded in the soft sand. To our great relief, Peter Sworder turned up in a tracked vehicle and offered to give us a tow. In a few minutes we were on our way heading east towards the rising sun. We had no idea how far back our own troops were with the tanks of the 2nd Armoured Brigade, or even the whereabouts of the German tanks. We could only travel hopefully and keep our eyes skinned.

Peter Sworder was a London wine-merchant by profession. As with most of the more senior officers he had started in the ranks of the HAC as a territorial soldier. As nearly all our members were potential officers the standard of those selected to be commissioned in the regiment was very high, so Peter was a splendid soldier and became a battery commander. He was thick-set, fair-haired, going bald, with a ruddy complexion.

He was fairly rough-tongued and did not suffer fools gladly, but underneath a rather cynical exterior he was kindly and warm-hearted. In battle he remained extremely calm, and the greater the danger the calmer he became. He won the MC at Knightsbridge where he was seriously wounded. He has remained a lifelong friend and I have had the privilege of christening his daughters and also some of his grandchildren.

We had not had any breakfast, or even our early morning brew-up, and after driving for about an hour, with no sign of any pursuit, Peter said, "Let's stop for breakfast." Looking over my shoulder, I rather anxiously said, "Shouldn't we drive on a bit further? The Germans can't be far behind us." "No," said Peter, "I want some breakfast. If we are going to be put in the bag (a polite way of referring to becoming a prisoner of war) we might just as well have full stomachs. The Germans are not likely to give us breakfast." He sat down in his camp chair, in the early morning sun, while we brewed up tea and bully on the desert fire, made as usual, with petrol and sand. There was no shortage of either. We felt much better after that as we had had very little to eat or drink during the hectic events of the last twenty-four hours.

We later heard that Major Jeff Linton, who was in charge of our party, had gone back to our night laager to see that everyone had managed to get away, and was immediately captured by the Germans. He later made a brave escape from a prisoner of war camp in Italy, and won the DSO at Arnhem. A very gallant soldier.

The next few days were very hectic. We heard later that Rommel's tanks had been engaged by the tanks of the 2nd Armoured Brigade and, in spite of the bravery of the regiments, Rommel had heavily defeated them. Our Cruiser tanks and Honeys were heavily outgunned by the more powerful German tanks, which could outrange them by a thousand yards. This defect was not remedied until the battle of Alamein, when we were equipped with the American Sherman tanks with their bigger guns and thicker armour. It took us nearly a week to get back to the safety of our main body established in front of Tobruk.

Each night, when we tried to get some sleep, we wondered whether it would be our last night of freedom. We depended on our vehicles not breaking down and the replenishment of our supplies of water and petrol.

On about the fourth day, our fifteen-hundredweight truck started making queer noises and something was clearly wrong. We stopped and after an examination, Mike Page announced that the track-rod had broken and we could not possibly repair it. While we were sadly contemplating a long walk with all our kit in the inhospitable desert heat, suddenly someone said, "Look, isn't that a stationary truck?" We looked, and in the distance, saw what might be a bush or an abandoned truck. It was often difficult to differentiate between them in the shimmering sunshine.

When we came up to it we saw that it was indeed an abandoned truck. We tried the engine and it started up immediately. Why had it been abandoned? On closer examination, we noticed that the radiator had been pitted with holes, probably from machine gun fire, and there was no water in it. Apart from that, it seemed in perfect order. If we could repair the radiator, it would probably go all right. We had very few tools but Mike was an excellent improviser and it was our only lifeline.

We had a glut of army biscuits. Mike pounded them into a paste with water and we pushed the gooey mixture into the holes in the radiator. We fortunately had enough water to fill the radiator, and hopefully we started up the engine. The heat of the engine baked the paste hard and it remained firmly in the holes. The truck went for many weeks without further mishaps and we were saved our long walk.

We had several unpleasant moments before we got back to safety. One night I remember vividly. We were on the edge of a salt lake, near a place called Saunnu. Daylight was beginning to fail and we were drawing into our night laager when, to our horror, we saw a large German column closing in on our line of retreat. Quite obviously we could not stay there for the night. We were short of petrol and, athough we were fortunate enough to find a small dump, we had not sufficient for all the vehicles to cover the fifty miles' night drive that we reckoned we had to do to get clear of the German column.

We dumped all unessential kit and piled on to the trucks that had been filled with petrol. I had to leave behind some valuable pieces of camp equipment that I had carried with me for many miles. Rifles and machine guns were kept at the ready in case we came too near an enemy laager. After a hair-raising drive of about twenty-five miles in pretty rough going, we paused to give the drivers a break. I volunteered to act as one of the sentries. We had with us the Headquarters of the 1st Support Group, of which our beloved Richard Goodbody was now brigade-major.

As I patrolled around the column, I saw Richard in the command vehicle, poring over a map to plan the next stage of our night march. I tapped on the window. "What on earth are you doing, padre?" he said. "Defying the Geneva Convention and acting as a guard," I replied, much to his amusement.

After another two hours' drive, as dawn was breaking, we joined up with the remnants from other columns in a rare oasis called Charuba, where we found some of the purest water we had ever had. Most of the water we used was quite heavily salted, giving our tea a curious flavour. 'Charuba water' became most popular for our brew-ups.

On our way back to Tobruk, we encountered a strong Polish column at Mechili. They covered our retreat to the coast at Timimi and we finally arrived back to Gazala, where General Ritchie was building a defensive line in front of Tobruk. We were stationed in a valley called Sidi Muftah, which we later nicknamed 'Happy Valley'.

It was the pleasantest time of the year, rather like an early English summer. We were in a shallow valley about a mile wide between two escarpments. There were flowers in the valley and the scent of fresh grass. It only lasted for a short time before the weather became really hot and dried up all the vegetation, but it coincided with a lull in the fighting and enabled us to get our breath back before the next battle. I remember it as the most pleasant four weeks of all the time I spent in the desert.

It had been a very tough baptism of fire, nearly always against heavy odds, and besides losing a number of guns, the regiment had suffered a number of casualties. Among my particular friends, Hew Tompson and Slogger Armitage, two delightful young subalterns, had been killed, alongside several soldiers.

Hew had been badly wounded during one of the Stuka raids and died of his wounds in hospital. Slogger Armitage was killed manning a gun against a number of German tanks when most of the gun crew had been killed or wounded. Tishy Benson and Quentin Drage also manned a gun until it was overrun by enemy tanks. They were both wounded, but lay doggo feigning death until the tanks had driven past them. They later made a remarkable escape back to our lines. All three deserved to be highly decorated for their bravery, but few decorations were awarded after a defeat. The men I had travelled with for over a month had been captured, and many of them lost their lives when the ship that was carrying them to Italy was torpedoed by one of our own submarines.

In spite of these disasters, morale in the regiment remained high. The fellowship that developed through facing dangers and tribulations together, was to prove of great value as the batteries, supplied with fresh guns and equipment, prepared for the next test of strength.

One of the most difficult sermons I had to preach to the regiment was on our return from our first taste of battle. We had gone in with high hopes. On the evening before we went into action, there was one of the most beautiful sunsets I had ever seen. The whole sky was lit up with a scarlet glow and the desert scene transformed into a place of magic and mystery. The presence of God was very real and our hearts were lifted up with a feeling of excitement and adventure. We returned rather deflated. We had been forced to flee from the enemy. We had lost a number of guns, a great disgrace to the Royal Regiment of Artillery. A number of our friends and comrades had been killed, wounded and taken prisoner. What could I say in such a situation?

While I was walking in the desert trying to prepare my sermon for Sunday, my foot hit something lying in the sand. I picked it up and saw that it was a belt with the inscription "Gott mit uns." It probably belonged to a German soldier killed in battle. He trusted in the same God that we did and I felt very close to Him in spirit.

Here was the theme for my sermon. God cares for all His children and those killed in battle, on whatever side, were safe in His loving hands. The crucified Christ faced the cruelty and evil of the world and built a bridge between man and God that remains firm in the midst of all the horrors and suffering of war.

Chapter Four

Desert Warfare

The time spent in Happy Valley remains one of my happiest recollections of the desert campaign. For the first time, I was given a vehicle of my own which gave me a feeling of independence and enabled me to move freely around the batteries who were scattered over a fairly wide area. My vehicle, a three-ton truck, became a mobile church and canteen and was a delight for Andy, who could now fulfil his role of "Padre's driver".

Church parades were over but, with small groups of men, I was able to hold regular informal services which consisted of simple prayers, a Bible reading, short address and a couple of well-known hymns. We had no musical accompaniment and the whole thing was delightfully informal. They were usually held early in the morning or as the sun was setting, since it was beginning to get very hot in the middle of the day. We were still under observation from enemy aeroplanes and, once of twice, when aeroplanes approached, I had to make a quick decision whether to continue the service or suggest that the congregation take cover. In each of the batteries I had a small group of regular communicants and have poignant memories of celebrating Holy Communion in a quiet wadi with a rock as an altar and half a dozen men standing round.

On one occasion during a service, an enemy plane

suddenly dived down and we heard a bomb explode very near. When I went back to the next group of soldiers, I found that the bomb had landed in the middle of the small camp and Gunner Hughes had been killed.

During this time we talked a great deal about the deeper side of life. We realised that some of us would be killed or wounded but never really imagined it would be ourselves. We talked a great deal about home. Food was also an important topic and anyone who could invent something new or exciting in our daily diet was most popular. My only contribution was some fish cakes made out of tinned salmon (a rare luxury from my canteen) and some mashed up army biscuits. We also discussed the coming battle and which commanders we were likely to have. We were too far away from divisional headquarters to know much of what was happening at that level, but the generals seemed to be changing over with great rapidity.

We were delighted when our Brigade Commander Raymond Briggs took over the division. He was an unusual character. It was rumoured that he had been a medical student. He was rather a hypochondriac and was always recommending some special pills to maintain health in the desert. Although he looked pale and delicate, he lived to a ripe old age and he has been a popular figure at our regimental reunions over the years. He was a splendid soldier and a very experienced tank commander. He played a notable part in the Battle of Knightsbridge commanding the 1st Armoured Division.

Now that I was mobile, with a large vehicle of my own, I suggested to the colonel that I might run a regimental canteen. We were still very restricted in our diet and a long way from any NAAFI stores. The colonel was delighted with the idea and I went round the batteries to discover what were the main requirements. Beer was at the top of the list; after that, cigarettes, chocolate and all kinds of tinned fruit. Anything to get away from the monotony of bully beef, tinned meat and vegetables, and army biscuits!

We set off on our hundred mile journey back to the base to find what luxuries we could buy. In spite of the lack of roads, apart from the coast road, we could find our way quite easily on what was known as the Trig Capuzzo, the track back to the frontier, also called 'The Wire'.

We hit the coast road at Bardia, a delightful small port on the coast, which had been an Italian colonial town. Most of the villas had been damaged by shell-fire and had no furniture, but we managed to find one that offered very adequate accommodation compared with two months of sleeping out in the open. A bathe in the tiny harbour was a wonderful refreshment after many weeks without a proper bath. After a good bully beef stew, we had the best night's sleep for a long time. Up early in the morning and off to the NAAFI store. We loaded a great many crates of beer on the truck, as well as other supplies and goodies that we had not seen for many months.

As we set off on our long trek back to the regiment, we heard ominous crackling noises from our load. We looked in the back and found, to our horror, that the beer was dripping from a number of broken bottles in the crates. It was quite obvious that after a hundred miles of rough going on the desert track, our chances of getting much beer back to the camp were pretty slight. We went back to the NAAFI and I sent for the manager. I pointed out that we had a long journey over rough going and that some of the bottles were already broken. He was most sympathetic and said, "Would you like to change the bottles for canned beer?" "What on earth is that?" I asked. "Oh, it's the latest thing from America," he replied. I inspected the canned beer and found it was packed in neat tins and was quite ideal for rough travel. We quickly made the exchange and joyfully set off for the regiment. The canned beer was a tremendous success and seldom has the arrival of the padre been greeted with such enthusiasm.

The regimental canteen became a feature of the chaplain's duties and, although some poured scorn on the

"Holy Grocer", I knew I was making a valuable contribution to the welfare of the troops and their morale, while relieving an officer for more warlike duties.

Travelling on one's own in the desert was difficult with the lack of roads, villages and signposts, with a map showing grid-lines and nothing else. It was rather like navigating at sea. One had to take a compass bearing and have some idea of the number of miles one had to travel. Having completed the required number of miles and failed to find our objective, it was no use going on, that was the surest way to get lost. One had to cast around in all directions, as it was quite clear one's bearing on the sun compass had not been accurate.

The first time I had to make a journey on my own to take a service with an outlying unit, although it was only a journey of a few miles, I failed to find them and was only too relieved to get back to the camp from which I had started. The desert was so vast in the shimmering bright sunshine that even bushes looked like a collection of vehicles, and it was only too easy to lose one's way. It was a serious business to become stranded out in the blue and to run out of petrol, water and food. Several soldiers lost their way and perished in the desert.

Eventually, we became quite expert with our navigation and could manage long distances with confidence. At night we used the stars, which in many ways were easier than the sun. We developed an instinct for direction and even today, I automatically check my direction by the sun when I am on an unknown route.

During the three months' respite from battle, apart from one or two Jock Column forays, we made several trips to the base to get supplies and one exciting trip right back to Alexandria, a distance of nearly five hundred miles. On our trips to the base for supplies, we usually spent one night out on our own and put up in our favourite villa in Bardia.

The leave to Alexandria was a welcome break and we

took a party of soldiers with us. It was our first real leave since our departure from England nearly six months before. At Alexandria, we put up at the Toc H hostel and had the comfort of civilised meals, baths and beds with clean sheets and, of course, a chance of getting our filthy clothes properly laundered.

As I was the first officer to get leave, I was given a number of errands to fulfil, including a visit to the local bank to cash a number of cheques for my fellow officers. I found a branch of Barclay's DCO and handed the cheques to an Egyptian clerk. He looked at them with grave suspicion and queried them all. As I was getting more and more impatient, and the clerk more and more unco-operative, I spotted an obvious Englishman at the back of the bank. His face looked vaguely familiar. I beckoned to him and explained my problems. I said, "Your face looks familiar." He replied, "Were you at Christ's Hospital? So was I." We realised we were contemporaries at school. After that there was no more trouble about the cheques.

John Heavens, who was a year or two older than I was, became a good friend. He introduced me to another old school friend who was the bank's manager and was a great help in making me conversant with the many amenities of Alexandria. He had lived there for a number of years. It was an ideal place for leave and for a few days we forgot the war and the rigours of the desert, swimming, sailing, playing tennis and sampling a splendid selection of eating places. Dicky Dines and Alan Spender, at the Fleet Club, were also most hospitable and our leave passed all too quickly. Our only reminders of the war were the nightly air raids on the harbour but our experience of being bombed, out in the open desert, made us feel quite secure under a roof.

Soon, we were on our way back to the desert, the truck filled with luxuries for the regiment, unobtainable from the NAAFI. On our return journey, we ran into the divisional postal officer with a pile of letters for the regiment. He had lost his way and had no idea where the regiment was. We took him under our wing and were lucky enough to contact Brigade Headquarters, who gave us the map reference of the regiment. When we finally rejoined them we had a wonderful reception, not only because of our canteen luxuries, but also because of the letters. There had been no news from home for several weeks and this was always very bad for morale, especially as many of the soldiers were Londoners and there had been news of heavy air raids. News from home was so vital for the well-being of the soldiers that it was once said that morale in the army was spelt MAIL.

Soon after our return from leave, the regiment suffered a sad loss. 'H' troop, of four guns from 'E' Battery, had been attached to a Free French column on Jock Column duty. They had been surprised by a large number of German tanks and almost completely destroyed. Only a few survived to be taken prisoner. I went up with a party to inspect the site of the disaster and take a funeral service for the dead. We found the guns still in their original position; they had all been rammed by tanks. Nearby, we found the graves of those who had been killed on the guns, John Venning and nine soldiers. I said some prayers over the graves. We later heard details of this most gallant action which had enabled the Free French column to retire safely.

Pommeroy Colley, and most of the survivors, were taken prisoner but Jack Sewell managed to get the 'A' echelon away. General Koenig, the French commander, sent a most enthusiastic report on the action and recommended the award of the Croix de Guerre to the Troop. This was later awarded in extraordinary circumstances, over forty years later, although at the time it was refused by Headquarters on the grounds that the Free French were not an official government.

'B' Battery was concerned in another Jock Column a few weeks later and as I usually accompanied them into battle, the colonel gave me permission to go with them. We were still out on Easter Sunday and were under close observation from the enemy. There was no chance of taking a service, as any movement was liable to bring down fire, and in daylight we had to remain scattered because of the threat of attack from the air. I realised that my only chance of taking a service would be when we moved into close laager in the dark. I spent part of the day trying to learn as much of the Communion Service as I could, by heart, especially the Prayer of Consecration, as I knew I would not be able to have any light in the laager to read the service.

After we had eaten our evening meal, I passed the word around that I would be holding a Communion Service at my vehicle before we bedded down for the night. I put a white cloth on the bonnet of my truck and found some biscuits and some rough Italian wine; with these I celebrated our Easter Communion. It was a most moving service and a number of men, who did not normally come to Communion, attended. One of them said to me, "It was a great comfort in the dark and after a hard day under fire." It was an Easter Sunday I shall never forget.

The next morning, the Battery Commander, I think it must have been Peter Sworder, said to me, "Ken, will you take the 'A' echelon of soft-skin vehicles back to the regiment as we have heard that there is a large column of German tanks in the neighbourhood. I will follow you with the guns." I navigated them safely back to brigade Headquarters. I felt the Brigadier was rather surprised to find the padre in charge of the column!

A few weeks of comparative peace followed and we were once more stationed in 'Happy Valley,' soon to be the scene of some of the hardest fighting of the campaign. We realised it was only the calm before the storm and that both sides were preparing for another decisive battle. We were establishing stronger defensive positions at Gazala, Knightsbridge and Bir Hacheim. This last was occupied by the Free French Brigade.

The weather was now hotting up, but every now and again we were surprised by a sudden and unexpected rain storm which turned the desert into a quagmire. We encountered one of these when we were returning alone from one of our expeditions to renew our canteen supplies. We were driving along a beautifully smooth part of the desert, and suddenly the storm broke. In a very short time the wheels of the truck were completely bogged down. As the rain continued to pour down, we took shelter under the canvas covering of the truck. As far as I can remember, Andy and I were accompanied by two other soldiers. When the rain stopped, we looked out from our covering and we appeared to be parked in the middle of a vast lake. As far as we could see, the whole desert was covered with a sheet of water. With our heavily loaded three-ton truck, it was quite clear that, at the moment, there was no chance of moving; we were absolutely stranded. We made ourselves as comfortable as we could and settled down for the night in the truck. Fortunately, we had no shortage of food or water. We cooked ourselves an unusually palatable meal from the canteen luxuries we had just purchased. This helped us to have a good night's sleep in spite of the precarious situation we were in.

We were many miles away from the regiment and, as far as we knew, no other units were in the vicinity. The wheels of the truck were completely stuck and we had no idea how soon we would be able to move. No one fancied a long walk, carrying all our belongings on our backs, and abandoning the truck with all its luxuries on board.

The next day, the sun shone but the waters showed no signs of abating. There was not much to do apart from enjoying our meals. There was no sign of life or movement, everything was still and silent. It was at times like these that the beauty of the desert became apparent. We discussed life in the desert of the nomadic arabic tribes we still encountered from time to time. We realised they led very much the same kind of existence as the ancient patriarchs of Israel whose lives are so vividly portrayed in the Book of Genesis. We also suggested that our experience of being bogged down by a sudden rain storm might explain what actually happened to the chariots of Pharaoh as they pursued the Israelites under Moses at the Red Sea. The Israelites could have crossed on foot while the chariots of Egypt became bogged down in the same way that we had been; an interesting theory that opened up a fascinating discussion and helped us pass the day and forget our predicament.

The next morning, the waters had subsided but the truck was still firmly bogged down in the sand and all our efforts to move it proved abortive. While we were gloomily contemplating another day and night of inactivity, we saw another truck approaching. As it came nearer, it seemed to be manned by foreigners and, for an awkward moment, we wondered whether they were Germans. However, to our great relief, they turned out to be Poles who assured us that the desert was now drying up and that movement was possible. The Poles had mastered enough English to make conversation easy. They were part of a small contingent who had escaped from the Russian invasion of their country and managed to get to the Middle East via the Balkans and Greece. It must have been a most exciting story. With their help we managed to drag our vehicle out of the sand and get the wheels clear. We were soon bowling along quite happily, and in a couple of hours rejoined the regiment, none the worse for our dampening experience.

Meanwhile, we sadly said goodbye to our colonel, "Baron" Ebbels, who had commanded us since 1940 and had proved an inspiring leader, whose unfailing courage and cheerfulness had nursed us through our first experience of real battle with all its sad losses, both in friends and in guns. He was promoted brigadier and became CRA of the newly formed 10th Armoured Division. Our ways met again a few months later when I became Senior Chaplain in the same division.

Chapter Five

Knightsbridge and its Aftermath

The months of March and April were the most pleasant times to be in the desert. The cold winds of January and February gave place to a pleasant warmth, and for a short time, flowers appeared and the desert was green. However, we knew it was only a temporary respite.

More equipment was being sent up from the base. Our cavalry regiments received some new American tanks, known as Grants, which were more heavily armoured than the Crusaders and carried a more powerful gun. Strong posts, known as boxes, were established at Gazala, Knightsbridge and Bir Hacheim. The latter, ten miles to the south, manned by the Free French, was supposed to be defence against a German attack on the flank.

On May 26th, Rommel moved to the south with his Panzer divisions and attacked at first light. In spite of previous warnings, he surprised and overran an Indian Brigade and the Headquarters of the 7th Armoured Division.

Rommel's attacks nearly always followed the same pattern. There was always an open flank away from the coast. Rommel moved at night and outflanked the whole of our position.

One of his columns attacked 7th Armoured Division on the south flank and another did an even wider sweep and attacked our supply lines at El Adem, a number of miles east of our main defences. He had two objectives, the destruction of the 8th Army and the capture of Tobruk which was about fifteen miles behind our main position. It was his failure to capture Tobruk in the previous year that had lead to his retreat to Agheila.

The next few days produced some furious fighting. After the early setbacks we had the better of the battles and it appeared that Rommel's attacks had been held. At one stage, he was cut off from his supplies and appeared to be on the edge of defeat. The opportunity was lost. A desert sandstorm sprang up obliterating the whole battlefield and was partly responsible for Rommel being able to readjust his forces.

The main problem on our side was the delay in making decisions. Rommel was always at the front and able to make quick decisions and concentrate his tanks and guns where they were most needed. Our commanders were too far in the rear and often at cross-purposes with each other.

Some years later, when the war was over, I had the opportunity of attending a senior officers' conference on the battlefield. Officers who had commanded squadrons, batteries and companies described the course of the battle from their point of view and it was quite clear that the main reason for our final defeat was lack of decision among our generals and their failure to concentrate strong enough forces where they were most required. This enabled Rommel to destroy the various strong positions one by one. The overwhelming of Bir Hacheim was one of the turning points of the battle.

My own impressions of the battle are very confused. Our regiment was split up in support of the three cavalry regiments. I still had my clumsy canteen three-ton truck and was supposed to be stationed with one of the 'A' echelons bringing up supplies of ammunition, petrol and rations as required. There was no fixed front line and the fighting was spread over a very wide area.

In the middle of the day, owing to the intense heat,

everything quietened down and in the evening we still managed to get some peace in our night laagers, in spite of a few raids from enemy planes.

During a lull in the battle, I made a trip into Tobruk to replenish my canteen supplies. The people there were anxious for news of the battle, as rumours of both defeat and victory, were rife. I assured them that at the moment all was going well. When I returned to the battle, everything had changed dramatically. Bir Hacheim had been captured and, in a fierce tank battle, our losses had been considerable. Our cavalry regiments were reduced to a third of their original number and, although the Grant tanks had given Rommel an unpleasant shock, his new Mark IV tanks had proved superior both in hitting power and armour.

Our anti-tank guns were still mostly two-pounders, with a very limited, effective range, although we were beginning to receive supplies of the much more satisfactory six-pounder. Attacks by Stukas, flying in from Crete, often caused heavy casualties. 'B' Battery lost a number of experienced men in one particularly savage attack.

During the Knightsbridge battle it was very difficult to decide where I ought to be. Apart from the boxes there was no front line and everyone was constantly on the move. The regiment was split up between the three armoured regiments and were continually being ordered to different positions as the situation demanded. No one had a very clear idea as to what was happening.

It was not always possible for me to keep close to the guns when they were dug in, as my three-ton truck was liable to attract enemy fire. At night as the fighting died down we usually went into close laager and were able to get some idea of what had happened during the day. Whenever possible, I tried to attach myself to the MO's truck as I felt I could be of some use in attending to the wounded. This was not always easy, as the MO's truck was forever on the move following the course of the fighting. It was only towards the end of the battle, when the regiment's remaining guns came together, that we were both able to link up with the regiment during its last desperate stand on the Acroma ridge.

We did become hardened to the sight of death and wounds. There was always so much to do and so much constant movement that I had little time to think philosophically of the implications of life and suffering and death. This came afterwards.

One vivid recollection was on my birthday, June 13th. We had just had our midday break of bully-beef, biscuits and tea, when we saw a dozen or more enemy planes flying in from the sea. It was a bright sunlit day and the planes were clearly outlined against the blue sky. The next moment they were diving straight at us and we could see the bombs being released. We yelled, "Take cover," and fortunately found some splendid slit trenches very near. Andy and I dived for them and I found myself lying on top of him. The noise of the bombs bursting all around us was appalling and it was followed by the planes diving to complete their work with machine guns. It seemed quite impossible for anyone to survive but our slit trenches had been skilfully constructed and no one was hit. A happy birthday!

The next day saw the last stand of the 8th Army in front of Tobruk. The regiment concentrated its remaining guns on a ridge at Acroma, which we knew well, and gave support to the few remaining tanks of the brigade. We appeared to be under fire all day and, as usual, whenever I could, I linked up with John Martin, our gallant regimental doctor.

At one point in the fighting, when the shelling was particularly fierce, we decided to seek the protection of the slit trench. We were crouching down when a truck drew up and out stepped John McDermid, the battery commander. He appeared perfectly calm, cool and collected and, rather sheepishly, John and I climbed out of the trench to greet him. He was an old friend and quite one of the bravest men I ever met. Later on, in the retreat, he was badly wounded and lost an eye. He never received any decorations for the wonderful example of courage and skillful leadership he displayed during the whole of that battle. Characteristically, several of the officers of his battery were awarded the Military Cross on his recommendation, but his own efforts went unrewarded.

As evening came on, the last surviving box on our left was overrun and I went forward in my truck and managed to rescue some men from the Worcester regiment who were retreating on foot.

The same afternoon, 'F' troop were overwhelmed by German tanks but went on firing until every gun had been hit. Major Hopkins, who had already won a MC and bar, drove up and rescued the gun crews. As he was driving back to our lines, he was hit by a shell splinter and immediately killed. Another most gallant officer.

As darkness fell, we knew we had managed to keep the coast road open and enabled many men from the Gazala line to get back to Tobruk in safety. However, our own line of retreat had been cut and we were ordered to leave our remaining guns and vehicles behind and scramble down the steep escarpment to safety. It was considered impassable to vehicles. John McDermid refused to accept this and was determined not to leave his guns behind. By sheer determination and brilliant driving, the guns and remaining vehicles were taken down the escarpment and up the steep slope opposite. Every gun and vehicle arrived at the coast road and drove safely to Tobruk.

I missed this wonderful feat as, a few hours earlier, I had been asked by the MO to take three ambulances full of badly wounded back to the hospital at Tobruk, before the road was cut. The coast road was packed and we had a nightmare drive back to Tobruk. We finally arrived at the hospital at about midnight and handed the wounded over.

It was quite impossible to get back to the regiment and my own truck.

I had my sleeping-bag with me, and looking around for somewhere to sleep, I found a handy balcony and dropped down, dead to the world. After what seemed a very short time, I was awakened by the sound of female voices. I discovered I had parked myself on the balcony of the nurses' quarters! The nurses had just been ordered to leave Tobruk in case there was another siege.

I managed to get a cup of tea and some breakfast and set off on foot to try and rejoin the regiment. I had no idea where they were but assumed they were still west of Tobruk. There was a feeling of panic in the town and no one seemed to know where the enemy were. Suddenly, I saw a three-ton truck approaching from the east. To my astonishment, I saw the driver was Andy. "Thank goodness I found you," he said, "The regiment is ten miles the other side of Tobruk and they are about to prepare for another seige. Unless we are quick, we shall be caught inside." Later, I discovered that he disobeyed orders in coming back to find me as he realised that otherwise I would have been trapped in Tobruk. When Tobruk fell a few days later, I realised that he had saved me from becoming a prisoner of war. He was indeed a most faithful and reliable friend. Thus ended the Battle of Knightsbridge. The regiment had won the unstinted admiration of all those who had fought with them. Often under the most difficult circumstances and facing the superior weight of German Panzer divisions, all ranks had behaved with the utmost gallantry. They had suffered heavy losses, twenty officers and two hundred and ten other ranks killed and wounded. They were almost the last formation to remain on the field of battle and their final action at Acroma had enabled many hundreds of men to avoid being captured and live to fight another day.

General Sir Gifford Martel wrote of the battle, "Although we suffered a severe defeat, there was some magnificent fighting. The 11th (HAC) RHA who fought with 2nd Armoured Brigade throughout the battle, achieved a magnificent record."

The next ten days were hectic and unsettling. Although, at the time no one realised it, we were about to embark on a 400-mile retreat back to Alamein. The depleted regiment was quickly reorganised on a two-battery basis, with Major John McDermid commanding 'A', and acting Major Geoffrey Armstrong in charge of the remnants of 'B'/'E'. 1st Armoured Division had been withdrawn to refit, so we came under 50 Division.

The news of the fall of Tobruk was a great blow. We next expected to make a stand on the Egyptian frontier at Sollum, but there were no prepared defences and, once more, Rommel outflanked us. The next possible position was at Mersa Matruh, and once more the guns took up positions to cover the retreating army. Twice they were cut off and twice they had to break through the German night laagers in thrilling night drives. Casualties were heavy, and during one of the drives, John McDermid was badly wounded and lost an eye.

He had played a magnificent part in those hazardous times and had proved himself an inspiring leader. He was our senior major and would have been a most inspiring CO of the regiment, but unfortunately he was evacuated to England on a hospital ship. A great loss to us all.

The adjutant, Arthur Green, was captured while attending to a wounded man. I missed him very much as a staunch Christian, a most competent adjutant and one of my first friends in the regiment. He was one of the many I had married before we sailed.

During most of the retreat, I was separated from the guns and travelled with 'A' echelon. We too had our share of adventures, some amusing and some rather frightening. One of the more amusing ones was the discovery of a NAAFI dump about to be evacuated by its attendants, who were not usually to be found so near the front line. As it was clear that anything we did not take would soon be seized by the Germans, we filled the truck with many delicacies that the troops in the front line seldom enjoyed. Tinned tongue and asparagus, tinned fruit of many different varieties and bottles of Guinness, chocolates, sweets and even new hair brushes. Andy said it was one of the most enjoyable days he had ever spent in the army, and when we rejoined our column, we felt like Father Christmas distributing presents to all and sundry.

One night we found a very pleasant beach just outside Mersa Matruh and settled down to have an evening meal before bedding down for the night. We had just lit our petrol fires and started to brew up when, in the distance some other vehicles reappeared. Someone shouted, "German armoured cars." We had no guns capable of dealing with them and the only thing we could do was to douse our fires, pack up our supplies and drive eastwards to safety.

Ron Norwood was our mechanical engineer, an expert in the care and maintenance of all our many and varied vehicles. Although not officially a member of the regiment, he soon became an integral part of the team. He had the great ability of making himself comfortable wherever he was, and in the desert his slit trench was always well equipped. He became a full member of the regiment and is still one of my most valued friends. He appeared to be an incorrigible bachelor and it was a great surprise when, a few years after I had left the army, he rang me up and asked if I would organise his wedding, which I very gladly did.

Ron, often my companion in adversity, and I made sure that everyone was clear of the site (in fact I had never seen a column pack up so quickly) and then acted as rearguard. It was a bright moonlit night and the road seemed fairly clear. Several times we heard enemy aircraft overhead: the Royal Air Force had protected us splendidly during daylight hours but at night there were still enemy planes about.

After driving all night, we finally arrived at what became known as the Alamein Line. To us it appeared to be just another piece of desert but we were assured that it was the last line of defence and that here the 8th Army must make its final stand. For an hour or two there was no sign of the guns or the remainder of the regiment and we feared they had been cut off by the enemy.

However, gradually they began to appear, the first ones convinced they were the only survivors. Gradually, more and more began to trickle in. It was quite clear that they had had the greatest difficulty in breaking out and had been surrounded by the Germans many times. Eventually, we numbered about 150 out of our full complement of over 700.

Six guns had been saved. The HAC, temporarily under 50 Div., was given the whole of the 50 Div. Artillery: viz. one 25-pounder, a troop of Bofors and part of a battery of two-pounder anti-tank guns, plus one officer who literally deserted. Geoff Armstrong appeared to be the senior surviving officer and he told me that General Auchinleck, now in command, had told him personally to be ready to stand on the Alamein line where he expected Rommel to make a final attempt to break through. If Rommel were successful, it would mean the loss of the whole of Egypt and a clear way through to all the Middle East oil. But in spite of its defeat at Knightsbridge and the long retreat back, the 8th Army was still intact and prepared to battle on to the end.

Geoff Armstrong told me he was worried over the absence of the colonel, who had got back safely with the survivors and to whom he had reported our depleted state. But the colonel had got back into his car and driven straight on to Alexandria, after ordering him to report to the CRA at 50 Div HQ. There, Armstrong was ordered to take the Division's remaining guns back into the line at daybreak. As we were going into action the next morning, he felt that the colonel should be with us. Would I go into Alexandria and try to find him? It was not an easy assignment as I ranked only as a captain, but I was the only one who could undertake such a delicate operation.

I snatched a few hours' sleep and set off with Andy in my battered old three tonner, at five in the morning. It was about a two-hour drive and I arrived at the leading hotel at about seven. I looked up the room list and found the colonel's name. When I went up to his room and explained why I had come for him, he was very angry and said 150 men did not justify the presence of the colonel. I told him that when the regiment went into action, they expected the colonel to be with them. He then said, "Come back at lunch time and I will come with you."

After lunch, we set off and arrived in time to find the regiment, with its six guns plus 50 Division's last 25-pounder, lined up and ready to join in the final defence of the Delta. The colonel wished them luck and said he was going back to the reinforcement camp to organise fresh troops to bring the regiment up to strength. He ordered the MO and myself to return with him. After two days in camp, the MO and I asked permission to go up to the line to visit the gunners. He agreed and said, "You can stay up for a day or two if you wish." We went up and had the honour of being with the regiment as they played their vital part in repelling Rommel's last frenzied attempt to break through.

In spite of continual requests and commands from the colonel for us to return to the base camp, we preferred to stay with the guns until the Alamein Line had been firmly established. It was a most exciting and exhilarating time. When I had a visit from the Assistant Chaplain-General of the 8th Army, I took him up to the gun position and he had the thrill of witnessing our seven guns firing at enemy tanks.

The disasters of the previous battles were forgotten and we felt we were avenging those of our comrades who had fallen during those past months. We were much heartened by the magnificent support we received from the RAF. No more diving into slit trenches when we saw an aircraft overhead. We knew it would be one of ours.

In this encounter, our casualties were light, though Robin Smith, who with Gerry de Boinville, had shown outstanding courage and skill in the forefront of the battle, was wounded with two other ranks. Both Robin and Gerry had been awarded MC's for their gallantry.

Eventually, with the guns almost worn out by their continual firing, the order was given to return to the Delta. Their task had been completed, Egypt was saved, the foundations had been laid for Rommel's final defeat. We had been in action, almost continuously, for fifty-seven days and overall had suffered grievous casualties.

The final tribute came from Brigadier Waller, under whose command we had fought the last battle. When saying farewell to Geoff Armstrong, he said, "The best trained battery I have ever seen. I hope I shall have the honour to serve with the HAC again." That, from a regular gunner to a territorial regiment, was praise indeed.

This was the turning point of the war for the British Army. Thereafter, until the end of the war, no battery of the regiment ever retreated. It was, sadly, also the last battle in which I served with them. The regiment under Geoff Armstrong had played a notable part in preventing Rommel from completing his victory and invading the Delta.

We returned to Cairo and marched through the city to the cathedral for a memorial service in honour of our comrades who had made the supreme sacrifice.

The joys of leave and the flesh-pots of the Delta were marred by internal troubles in the regiment, caused entirely by the behaviour of the colonel. Owing to his influence at Middle East Headquarters, where he had served for several years before joining the regiment, he was able to arrange for Geoff Armstrong to be transferred to base. Geoff had refused his invitation to be second in command, as he was hoping instead to command 'A' Battery. He had shouldered the burden of leadership during those last vital weeks when the colonel had preferred to remain at the base, during which time he had won the affection and admiration of all of us who had served under him. He was a superb soldier and a skilled and accomplished gunner. After he left us, he had a most distinguished career and won the DSO when commanding a gunner regiment in Burma. His transfer almost caused a mutiny amongst the officers.

All the surviving members of 'A' Battery asked for a transfer, which was granted. Thus, the regiment lost a number of experienced officers who had proved themselves in battle. The officers in 'B' and 'E' Batteries, who felt equally strongly, were told that the regiment would be disbanded if they too asked for transfers.

I felt I was in an extremely difficult position, as I found it impossible to respect the colonel or serve him loyally. I requested an interview with the Deputy Chaplain-General and explained my position. He was very sympathetic and understanding. I told him I was not asking for a transfer, but if there was an opportunity of a posting to an active formation, perhaps he would consider me. I was determined not to remain at the base when the regiment went back to the line.

During this time, I had a short spell in hospital. A slight wound in my arm had been aggravated by neglect and dirt and had developed into what were known as "desert sores". John Martin, our MO, suggested that a spell in hospital would soon put me right. After a week, I was so much better that when Ron Norwood came to visit me and suggested that Robin Smith, who was recovering from a leg wound, and myself should go out to tea with him, the ward sister readily agreed. We went down to the officers' club alongside Lake Timsah, where there were a number of sailing dinghies. Ron offered to take us for a sail, but as soon as we embarked, it was clear that his knowledge of sailing was minimal. Robin and I suggested we should return to the safety of the shore. As Ron tried to turn the boat around, we were struck by a sudden squall and capsized. We managed to cling to the upturned hull until Roger Croxton, who was a skilled yachtsman, came out in another boat and rescued us. When we got back to the hospital we had a good deal of trouble explaining to the ward sister why our uniforms were so wet! We were discharged from hospital the next day.

A month later I was promoted Senior Chaplain to the 10th Armoured Division. Andy, of course, came with me. I did not ask permission as I knew it would have been refused, but the regiment regarded us as a team and I knew he would be welcomed with open arms by the 10th Armoured Division, as experienced drivers were highly prized, and once we were under their command, Andy's transfer was regularised. It was with great sadness that I said farewell to my many friends with whom I had experienced so much. Fortunately, I retained my membership of the HAC and am still their Honorary Chaplain over forty years later.

I had been with them through all the training period, when losing so many of their original members, they had absorbed an astonishing variety of recruits from every walk of life and embued them with the great traditions of the regiment. This tradition combined the ancient voluntary spirit of the HAC with the regular army tradition of the Royal Horse Artillery, with its pride in the guns and quick action. This combination was enshrined in the title 11th (HAC) RHA. It was this spirit that enabled the regiment to endure the early disasters of the Jock Columns, and to fight with such tenacity through the gruelling disappointment and defeats of Knightsbridge, to maintain its cohesion through the 400-mile retreat to Alamein, which twice involved breaking out of enemy encirclement, and in spite of over 500 casualties, to produce a battery that played an outstanding part in preventing the German army from breaking through into the Delta and the Middle East oil fields.

I treasure the memories of the magnificent spirit of comradeship that made these achievements possible. Officers and men lived at close quarters and shared the hardships of desert life: the shortages of food and water, the lack of material comforts, the rigours of the climate, ranging from cold biting winds to intense heat. I remember the tender care for the wounded, the sympathetic understanding for those few whose nerves broke under the strain of battle and the courage that gained the regiment so many decorations: three DSO's, two DCM's, nineteen MC's and 16 MM's, and countless deeds of heroism that went unrewarded.

It was a wonderful privilege to have served as chaplain to such a magnificent body of men. They were not far from the "Kingdom of Heaven."

A few months after I had left them, I was delighted to hear that the colonel had been replaced by our beloved Richard Goodbody; an appointment that thrilled everyone and soon restored to the regiment its ancient spirit.

Epilogue

The role of a senior chaplain at divisional headquarters was rather different from that of a regimental chaplain. My first responsibility was the placing of chaplains to the various regiments of the division and ensuring that all the units had a chaplain they could call on. This was made difficult by the fact that there were never enough chaplains to go round and also that each division had its quota of Roman Catholic and Free-Church chaplains. The proportion was usually about ten C of E, three RC and three Free-Church, who might be Methodist, Presbyterian or Baptist. In the last resort it was not the denomination of the chaplain that mattered but his character and personality.

A good chaplain would stay with the same regiment for a long time; an indifferent one was constantly on the move. My heart always fell when a chaplain was sent to the division with a long list of previous postings, as I realised no one really wanted him.

My other main task as a senior chaplain was to get to know the general and the unit staff officers and to win their confidence. It was equally important to make contact with the CO's of all the regiments in the division and to make sure they were happy with their chaplains and were giving them full support.

A chaplain could be very lonely in a regiment, and I felt

it was very important to build the chaplains into a team and develop a strong fellowship amongst them. In many ways this was my most satisfactory task as senior chaplain. I was very fortunate in having as the chaplain at divisional HQ a most delightful young Methodist, Marcus Taylor. He was one of the youngest chaplains in the army, very goodlooking with dark wavy hair and a most charming smile. He had been with the division for some time and knew all the other chaplains. He was a great help in welding them into a team as he had a wonderful gift for friendship. During my time with the division, we lived and worked together and our friendship continued for many years after the war. He eventually became an Anglican priest.

When I joined the division in September 1942, we all knew that a vital battle was very near. Since I left the HAC, a new general had arrived to command the 8th Army. Many accounts have been written about the dramatic effect the arrival of General Montgomery had on the 8th Army and the story is now widely known. In a few weeks he completely transformed the spirit of the Army and by his victory at Alam Halfa had demonstrated his mastery of the battlefield. It was no longer just a case of hanging on at Alamein, we felt confident that we could defeat Rommel.

One of Monty's greatest gifts was the choice of his staff. Once he decided on a soldier's ability he backed him to the hilt. His choice of his chief chaplain was a typical example. The Rev'd Freddie Hughes had been vicar of Mansfield before the war and a territorial chaplain. He had come out to Palestine with the Cavalry Division and had become their senior chaplain. This was the basis of the 10th Armoured Division when the regiments lost their horses and became mechanised with tanks and armoured cars.

It was Freddie's promotion to a Corps HQ that brought me to 10th Armoured. When I reported to the General he said, "Padre you have a very difficult job, you are replacing one of the best chaplains I have ever met."

Monty obviously thought the same, as in a very short time he had appointed Freddie as the senior chaplain of the 8th Army, a double jump of promotion.

When Monty left the 8th Army to become Commander-in-Chief of the Normandy invasion force, he took Freddie with him and they remained together until Freddie became Chaplain-General, and Monty Chief of the Imperial General Staff.

When Freddie told Monty that the chaplains' work was greatly hindered by the shortage of transport, Monty at once ordered that every chaplain in the 8th Army must be issued with his own truck, so that before the final battle of Alamein began, every chaplain was properly equipped and mobile. It was a great boost to our morale as it made us feel that our work was really appreciated. Monty never went into battle until he was convinced that he had all the necessary ingredients for victory.

He once said "I would as soon go into battle without my artillery than without my chaplains." A great compliment to us.

The 10th Armoured Division played a significant part in the great victory of Alamein and the chaplains came out of the battle with great credit, winning two MC's and several "mentioned in despatches."

It was rather a disappointment when we were withdrawn from the advancing army soon after we had reached Mersa Matruh, but there were obvious advantages of spending Christmas among the flesh-pots of the Delta. I was fortunate enough to be selected for a chaplains' refresher course in Jerusalem and had the thrilling experience of a tour of the Holy Land.

The Bishop of Jerusalem, in full episcopal regalia, and the cathedral choir met us at the station. He greeted us warmly and announced that he proposed to march with us around the walls of Jerusalem singing psalms. As we had come straight out of battle and had a long and uncomfortable train journey, I suggested we might first have a bath and a rest. The dear bishop replied, "The first pilgrims who came to Jerusalem had walked all the way from England and yet they sang psalms on arriving." So of course we sang psalms too! A few months later I managed to arrange to take a party of a hundred and fifty soldiers on a similar tour.

After spending Christmas in Cairo, the division was ordered to join the 9th Army in Syria. It was hoped to persuade Turkey to come into the war, and the presence of a fully equipped armoured division on her frontier might be an encouragement.

Syria, after a brief battle with the Vichy French, was now a peaceful country and we spent almost a year there exploring her fascinating historical remains, the beauty of the Lebanese mountains and becoming accustomed to moving an armoured division in mountainous country, a great contrast to the desert. We expected our next battles would be fought in Italy.

During the winter we were stationed around Aleppo, an ancient city composed of both Christian and Islamic quarters. We made friends with some Armenian Christians and had the use of a splendid church. Here we had some of the most memorable voluntary services we ever managed to hold in the division. A fine choir was composed of male voices from the soldiers and female voices from the very attractive Armenian girls.

We normally had the more formal church parades in the morning and voluntary services in the crypt in the evening. During Holy Week we sang Stainer's *Crucifixion.* We had several experienced choirmasters including Douglas Robinson, who after the war became chorus-master at Covent Garden Opera House.

On the welfare side, my main task was the establishing of a large canteen and recreation centre for the troops. It was named the Foxes' Mark after the divisional sign.

When the weather became hot, our general Horace Birks insisted on moving the division up into the mountains, and in spite of a number of difficulties, managed to keep us supplied at a height of over five thousand feet. The weather here was quite perfect and we were camping in a countryside of great beauty.

The Italian Campaign had begun meanwhile, so we were moved back to the Canal Zone to prepare to rejoin the 8th Army.

Unfortunately, it was decided that there was no requirement for another divisional HQ, so, much to our dismay, the division was broken up and the regiments despatched to Italy as independent brigades. I was very sad to say goodbye to the many friends I had made during the eighteen months we had been together, but the spirit of the Headquarters was so good that after the war we met together once a year in an "All Ranks" Reunion.

As all our friends were being posted to Italy, Marcus Taylor and I were determined to get posted there. After some trouble with the Chaplains' Branch at Middle East HQ, who were anxious to keep us there, we both achieved our objective.

I was appointed senior chaplain at 46 Infantry Division who were just about to sail for Italy, while Marcus, after an adventurous unofficial trip across the desert to Algiers, joined the 2nd RHA in Italy.

46 Infantry Division was commanded by General 'Ginger' Hawkesworth, one of the finest divisional commanders I came across. He never spared himself in battle and was a constant inspiration to the brigade and regimental commanders. At first sight he was rather austere and stern, but underneath he was warmhearted with a splendid sense of humour. He was a committed Christian and was always most concerned with the work of his chaplains. I was fortunate enough to be invited to live in 'A' mess with him largely because I could make up the bridge four which was his evening's relaxation after a

long day with the troops. Normally the chaplain would have lived in 'C' mess, much further away from the line. He was promoted to command a corps but sadly died on his way home as the result of a wound he had received in his head in the 1914 War.

The other outstanding personality in the division was Joe Kendrew who commanded the Hampshire Brigade. He had been a rugger international before the war and had displayed great skill and courage as a regimental commander. As a brigade commander he always led from the front and when a regiment was given an objective, its main fear was that the Brigadier might get there before them. He won three DSO's in the campaign and collected a fourth in Korea.

I had taken Andy with me, and the division was delighted that I had such an experienced batman-driver with me. After we landed at Taranto, the division took part in the Gothic line battle proceeding up the Adriatic coast to Rimini and Bologna. Being with an infantry division in mountainous country was a great contrast to the desert campaign. The Germans fought skillful rearguard actions, the mountains and rivers giving them excellent defensive positions.

The infantry regiments suffered a number of casualties, and during the battle my main job was organising divisional burial grounds to avoid the dead being buried in scattered graves. Before each battle I found out from the operational staff where the most severe fighting was expected to take place and did a recce for a suitable position. I then notified the regimental chaplains where they could bring back their dead. It was rather a dreary task especially as the main war was now being fought in France and we felt we were rather a sideshow.

At the end of the campaign, just before Christmas, the division was ordered to Greece. Having had over three years overseas, I was posted home to deal with some family troubles. Andy drove me down to the docks at

Naples and my last glimpse of him was standing at the gangplank giving me a farewell salute. He returned to 46 Infantry Division and came back to England a year later having had four years' devoted service overseas.

I had six months in England in Catterick Camp where I met a number of men who like me had served in the 8th Army.

The European War came to an end and, as both my brothers were in the Navy in the Far East, I volunteered for service overseas. I only got as far east as Baghdad where I was posted as Assistant Chaplain-General to the army in Persia and Iraq. I was very surprised to receive this double jump of promotion and I stayed in Baghdad until victory was finally won over Japan.

The Commander-in-Chief of Persia and Iraq (PIA Force) was Arthur Smith who had been Wavell's Chief of Staff. He was known throughout the army as an outstanding Christian and informed me on my arrival at his headquarters with a twinkle in his eye that he firmly believed that the whale swallowed Jonah.

When PIA Force was closed down, I returned for the third time to the Canal Zone, where I was in charge of a desert church called St Martins-in-the-Sands. We were largely concerned with the demobilisation of our own troops and also the repatriation of some eighty thousand German prisoners of war camped in the area.

Many of them were allowed out on parole to work in the camp, and I had both a German church orderly and a German driver. The orderly was a charming young Austrian boy called Rudolf, who decided to become 'C of E' while he was with us. I advised him to return to the Roman Church when he got back to Austria. Three years later, I took a troop of scouts to an international Jamboree in Austria and to my surprise and joy Rudolf turned up with his girlfriend having hitch-hiked from the Russian Zone. He spent the remainder of the Jamboree with us and I still have a Tyrolean hat he bequeathed to me when we were about to return to England.

The other memory of the Canal Zone was the return of my school Bible. I was organising the chaplaincy services in the POW camps and had discovered a number of anti-nazi ministers who had been conscripted in the ranks of the German army. We issued them with purple armbands and gave them our full support in organising the appropriate services for their denominations. At the end of my introductory talk one of them approached me and said "Did you say your name was Oliver? I think I have got your Bible. I recovered it from a captured British truck four years ago and have been learning English from it." I was overjoyed to have it back.

I returned to England at the end of 1946, again on compassionate grounds. My younger brother who had served with the Navy throughout the war, having survived the sinking of the *Ark Royal* and arduous voyages with Russian convoys and Japanese suicide attacks, was killed flying in the Fleet Air Arm. He left a widow and two children, the youngest being born after his death.

Towards the end of 1947, I was posted to Germany as senior chaplain to the 7th Armoured Division, the old Desert Rats. It was my first experience of service abroad in peacetime. In some ways it was much more like being a parish priest at home, as there were a number of families with the division. I arrived in Germany when the policy of non-fraternisation with the German people was being dropped as we realised we must try to help them return to democratic ways. Naturally those who had been involved in the atrocities of the concentration camps had to stand trial. We were very near Belsen and were only too conscious of the horrors and mass murders that had been perpetrated there. There is no doubt that the vast majority of the German people had been kept in the dark as to what went on in the concentration camps, although they must have been aware of the horrific campaign against the Jews.

We were stationed in the picturesque old town of Celle, which had great links with the former Hanoverian monarchs of England.

I called on the local minister, a Lutheran, and said we would like to invite some of his congregation to our services. He was delighted with the idea and later on we were invited to his church. We found the Lutheran services rather heavy going, but enjoyed getting to know some of the German congregation. I was invited to preach in his church and had the task of furbishing up my schoolboy German with the help of a German secretary. My sermon was a good deal shorter than my Lutheran colleague's!

A very welcome innovation to the chaplain's work at this time was the introduction of so-called "Church Houses". The authorities were most helpful and handed over three country houses to the chaplains where courses in Christian leadership could be run. It was quite clear that the churches at home would need a large number of ministers, as recruitment had been largely stopped during the war. It was the responsibility of the chaplains to seek out and encourage potential ordinands, and the Church Houses were ideal centres for this work.

The first courses were largely for committed Christians and those who were considering being ordained. Later on, the whole conception was enlarged and we found the Church Houses were ideal centres for more general Christian teaching.

National service was still in operation and the youth of the nation was still being drafted into the services. Many commanding officers were only too pleased to send numbers of these young soldiers to the Church Houses to attend Christian leadership courses. It was a challenge to the chaplains to make the courses sufficiently challenging and relevant to arrest and maintain the attention of youngsters, many of whom had never had any contact with the Church. The courses became sufficiently popular and well-known for many officers and NCO's to volunteer to attend. They usually lasted for two or three days and they gave the chaplain the opportunity of giving a series of comprehensive lectures on the Christian faith with plenty of opportunity for questions. Living together, eating together and worshipping together were equally as important as studying together. We received great help from visiting clergy from home, and we were particularly fortunate in having Cuthbert Bardsley, then Bishop of Croydon, as the forces' Bishop. He was an old friend of mine; we had passed out of theological college at the same time. He had a great gift of expounding the Christian faith lucidly and logically, and on a number of occasions he held the attention of a roomful of senior officers for almost an hour while he explained some of the basic beliefs of the Christian faith and their relevance for today. In many regiments, Padres' Hours were held which gave the chaplains the opportunity of answering the soldiers queries and expounding the Faith.

I had been in Germany for about a year, when I received a letter from Freddie Hughes, our Chaplain-General, asking whether I would like to come back to England as Warden of the Chaplains' Training Centre at Bagshot Park. I was very happy with 7th Armoured Division. We had a garrison church in Celle and a thriving worshipping community and choir and I had made a number of friends with the local Germans. I consulted my general and wrote back saying that I would rather stay with the division for the usual tour. Freddie Hughes then wrote back that, when he asked me if I would like to go, what he really meant was that he wanted me to go. So I went.

Bagshot Park had been built by Queen Victoria for her second son, the Duke of Connaught. It was a vast Victorian Gothic mansion set in a most beautiful park on the edge of the Windsor estate. After the war, King George VI offered it to the chaplains as a Depot and Training Centre. We had never had a depot of our own and Freddie Hughes had the imagination to see what a great asset it could be to the army chaplains.

There were still a number of new chaplains coming into the army to take the place of those who had been demobbed and our first priority was to arrange a three weeks' training course to give them some idea of the kind of conditions they would be meeting in the army. We fitted them up with the necessary uniforms and gave them basic instructions in drill, first aid and map-reading.

The second type of course was for potential ordination candidates who were still serving in the army and hoping to go on to theological training when they were demobbed. However, most courses were for the ordinary layman in the army, of all ranks from general to private. The very senior officers usually came for one day, but most of the other courses lasted for two or three days and were residential.

We came under the command of Eastern Command, and when I arrived, our general was Gerald Templer. He gave us complete support and offered to come on a day course with all his generals and brigadiers to see for himself what we were putting over. He was so delighted with the course that he at once gave orders that all the commanding officers should attend a similar course, followed by the leaders at all levels. This was a most exhilarating experience, not the least being a course entirely composed of sergeant-majors, many of them from the Guards. They were very surprised at finding themselves in a Christian leadership course but when they realised that we were not going to preach at them but try to answer some of their questions about Christianity, they responded with considerable enthusiasm and gained a greater understanding of what chaplains were trying to achieve.

The senior Regimental Sergeant-Major of the Brigade of Guards, a most formidable figure, on thanking us before he left, said, "I did not want to come on this course but I enjoyed it and I have learnt something. When I get back to my regiment I am going to be a better Christian, and the rest of the regiment are going to be better Christians as well!" A splendid man.

As with church houses in Germany and elsewhere we ran a number of courses for young national servicemen.

While I was there, we completed the building of a memorial chapel for those chaplains killed in the war. There were over a hundred killed in action, I believe a higher proportion than any other branch of the army.

I had as my chaplain, Canon Knox, a priest of great experience with a majestic appearance. He had played a great part in designing the chapel. When it was completed Field-Marshal Montgomery unveiled the memorial plaque and spoke in glowing terms of the work of the chaplains during the war.

Bagshot Park catered for all denominations in the army; the sub-warden there was a Methodist chaplain, Harry Breakespeare, who had been with me in Germany. He was ideal in every way and a great asset on the courses.

I spent three very happy and eventful years at Bagshot Park and always welcome the opportunity of returning there for reunions and retreats. It has become a vital part of the chaplains' work in the army.

In many ways it was quite different from normal army life, rather like returning to the academic world, a most useful experience.

My next posting was back to Egypt as Assistant Chaplain-General to the British troops there. There was still the equivalent of two divisions with a large amount of stores and base equipment.

We set sail on New Year's Eve 1951, and arrived at Port Said after a pleasant cruise through the Mediterranean. I found the situation in Egypt rather tense. There had been an army revolution and the generals in charge, first Neguib and later Nasser, were pressing for the evacuation of the British Army from the Canal Zone, in accordance with the assurance given by the Labour Government in 1946.

We had already given up our bases in Cairo and Alexandria. The headquarters were stationed in Moascar, a very pleasantly situated camp on the outskirts of Ismalia, halfway between Port Said and Suez. The garrison church was built in the style of an eighteenth-century English parish church and was quite one of the most attractive I had ever come across. We had a large number of families in the camp and the set-up was very much like a normal English parish.

The church was run by the garrison chaplain and my responsibility was the general oversight of all the army churches in Egypt of which there were about twenty. The Roman Catholics did not come under my control but we met them frequently and always invited them to the chaplains' conferences. There was a church house on the shore of Lake Ismalia and as usual we organised courses of Christian Leadership.

I became closely connected with the garrison church at Moascar. The chaplain was an old friend, whom I had married some years before. Ken Kendra and his wife Katie were most hospitable; their home was a welcome change from life in the officers' mess. My staff chaplain was a Presbyterian called David Henderson who was quite outstanding as an administrator as well as being a devoted minister. He and Rachel had a charming family of boys and I was equally at home with them as with the Kendras. It was a very happy posting.

One of the features of family life in the Canal Zone was the setting up of schools and activities for the young. Amongst these were a number of Boy Scout Troops. I had been connected with the Scout Movement for many years and was appointed District Commissioner for all the service scouts. We worked closely with the RAF who had a number of scout troops in their stations. Quite by chance we heard that the Chief Scout, Lord Rowallan was due to pay a visit to Greece to inspect the scouts there.

I at once wrote to Scout Headquarters and reminded them of the several hundred British scouts in Egypt and suggested that Lord Rowallan might come on to us, as Greece was fairly adjacent.

The reply came back that he was unfortunately on a very tight schedule and unless we could supply him with an aeroplane, it was quite impossible. They obviously thought that was the end of the matter. They were quite wrong. Our general Sir Francis Festing, later Field-Marshal, was an enthusiastic supporter of the Scout Movement. He was thrilled with the idea of a visit from the Chief Scout, and after a brief telephone conversation with the RAF Air Chief-Marshal, an aeroplane was soon arranged. The result was a mini-jamboree and a most successful visit from the Chief Scout.

The chaplains were encouraged to organise expeditions to places of interest in the locality and one of the favourite sites was St Catherine's monastery in the middle of the Sinai Desert. This was the traditional site where Moses received the tablets of the Ten Commandments. I was lucky enough to join one of these trips and had the thrill of climbing to the top of Mount Sinai.

Another feature of life in the Canal Zone was the number of sporting activities. I soon found myself involved in playing and helping to organise cricket, rugger, hockey, tennis and squash.

I was not actually still playing rugger but had become a very keen referee. I always found participating in games a very valuable means of getting to know soldiers of all ranks in a different setting from church. Cricket was a most popular game and we revived a famous Egyptian club known as the Five C's (Catch as Catch Can).

Two memorable occasions were a visit to Alamein, Tobruk and Knightsbridge, and the coronation of Queen Elizabeth II.

The first took place on October 23rd, the anniversary of the battle. We obtained special permission from the

Egyptian government to drive through the Delta but they insisted on providing an escort of security police who followed us about wherever we went, much to the general's fury.

We held a memorial service on the site of the Alamein memorial. We did the same at Tobruk, and I found the names of a number of members of the HAC whom I had buried in the desert. At Knightsbridge, the general held a full-scale recapitulation of that dramatic battle with accounts of what had actually happened on the ground from officers who had commanded squadrons, batteries and companies. One of the most illuminating was the description of the terrific defence of Bir Hacheim by the Free French given by the man who had been General Koening's Chief of Staff. It was a most moving experience for me to return to the place where the HAC had fought with such courage and suffered so many casualties.

It was quite clear that we had been defeated by Rommel's skillful use of his superior tanks and the dreaded 88 millimetre gun in spite of the bravery of our men.

Queen Elizabeth's coronation was marked by ceremonial parades and church services.

After nearly two years in Egypt, Tubby Clayton wrote and asked me how much longer I was going to stay in the army and whether I would consider succeeding him as Vicar of All Hallows Church in the city.

I was quite keen to come home after seven years abroad out of the last ten. Victor Pike had now become Chaplain-General and I wrote to him for advice. He replied that he would like me to come home to take charge of the Guards' Chapel. This was a most exciting posting as it involved not only running the Guards' Chapel but also being responsible for all the chaplaincy services in London including the Tower of London and the Royal Hospital at Chelsea, the Chelsea Pensioners. So I told Tubby Clayton that I expected to serve at least another three years in the army.

I did however retain my connection with Toc H by living at Mark II which was situated in St George's Square and was conveniently near the Guards' Chapel. There was a quarter available in the barracks but, as I was a bachelor, this was occupied by the regimental chaplain Ron Woods who was married with a family.

The services at the Guards' Chapel were accompanied every Sunday by the Guards' Band on duty and were always very well attended. In many ways it was similar to being in charge of a West End church and I thoroughly enjoyed being a member of the Westminster Rural Deanery which contained many famous churches and naturally a very distinguished group of clergy, several of whom subsequently became bishops. I had the great privilege of preaching in a number of these churches, including Westminster Abbey.

In return, I was able to invite a number of distinguished clergymen to preach at the Guards' Chapel, including Tubby Clayton who was delighted to renew his contact with the army.

I also invited my uncle, Bernard Oliver, a country parson who was vicar of Mayfield in Sussex for over forty years. His simple sermon straight from the heart and preached without a note made a great impression on my rather sophisticated congregation.

Church parades were now held only on special national and regimental occasions, and the chaplains' opportunity of presenting the gospel to the soldiers was through the Padres' Hours which had now become part of the normal army routine.

My greatest day at the Guards' Chapel was the Dedication of the Guards' war memorial which was unveiled by the Queen on a lovely summer day in St James's Park. It took the form of a cloister; this was the start of the re-building of the nave of the chapel which had been completely destroyed by a doodle-bug during one of the blitzes on London. The bombing had occurred on a

Sunday morning during morning service and nearly two hundred members of the congregation had been killed.

The cloister contained an alcove for each of the seven guards' regiments with a memorial book containing the names of the fallen. The service took place in St James's Park with the massed band of the Guards in the presence of nearly all the members of the Royal Family. I had the honour of conducting the service, and after the Chaplain-General had given the blessing, the Queen unveiled the memorial.

The BBC presented me with a recording of the service which is still one of my most cherished possessions.

That year, Remembrance Day, November 11th, fell on a Sunday and I was invited by ITV to broadcast evensong from the Chapel and the Cloister, one of the first services to be broadcast on ITV.

After three years at the Guards' Chapel, I received my last overseas posting to Singapore to be Assistant Chaplain-General of the army in South East Asia. Although General Templer had been successful in quelling the main communist revolt in Malaya, there were still a number of troops stationed there to eradicate the remaining nests of bandits in the jungle, and there were also garrisons in Hong Kong and Korea. It was a most exciting part of the world to be in and I spent half my time travelling over the whole area.

My main responsibility was to make contact with the chaplains serving in these garrisons, and also to ensure that the limited number of chaplains available were placed to the best advantage. I worked in close co-operation with the Bishop of Singapore, and whenever I was going on tour, I enquired whether there were any British civilians in out-of-the-way places he would like me to visit.

Apart from Hong Kong and Malaya, which I visited regularly during my time in the Far East, I visited Korea, where I dedicated the memorial to the Gloucester

Regiment on the borders of North and South Korea.

In Nepal, I travelled with the Bishop of Barrackpore to arrange the building of a church in the reinforcement camp of the Gurkhas. We had a fascinating trip through India, crossing the Ganges in a very ancient ferry. Later, I was asked by the Bishop to take a service in Saigon and from there on to Phnom Penh for a much delayed christening.

While I was in Phnom Penh I was lucky enough to be offered a flight to the temples of Ankor Wat. These are some of the most remarkable religious buildings in the world. Remaining undiscovered for several hundred years, they had been almost completely swallowed up by the jungle. They were unearthed during the French occupation of Indo-China. The French did a remarkable rescue job and when I went there in 1955, many of them, including the vast one at Ankor Wat, many times larger than Canterbury Cathedral, had been completely restored. At the present time, owing to the devastating war in Cambodia, they can no longer be visited. I am afraid many of them will again be engulfed by the jungle.

There was a large garrison in Singapore and a number of army churches. The main one, which was at Tanglin, the army headquarters, was a fine example of a garrison church, and extremely well attended, with a well-trained choir and many of the normal parish organisations.

There was a splendid Anglican cathedral in Singapore with a multi-racial congregation. I became an honorary member of the staff and regularly took part in the services. My wife and I visited it on our way to Australia a couple of years ago and were delighted to find a large congregation composed of many different nations, including British, Chinese and Indian.

In Singapore, I once more became involved in Scouting and Toc H. In 1959 there was an international scout jamboree in the Philippines and we were invited to send a contingent. In addition, a large party was sent out from

Great Britain and we were asked to entertain them, as Singapore was their last stop en route for the Philippines. I was requested to join them as chaplain and go on with them.

I was delighted to do this. It was an astonishing adventure, as the Philippines were not used to organising a camp for such large numbers from all over the world. The jamboree was only saved from being a complete disaster by the splendid spirit and adaptability of the visiting scouts.

After three exciting years in South East Asia I returned home at the end of 1959 and retired from the Army in 1960 at the end of twenty-one years' service.

I had made a number of friends, both chaplains and laymen in all ranks of the army and shall always be thankful for all the opportunities I was given. The support for chaplains is quite amazing and I can unhesitatingly recommend any young clergyman of whatever denomination to consider volunteering for service amongst some of the finest of his fellow-countrymen, in an organisation where the Christian virtues of service and fellowship are still highly regarded.

Before I left the army, my son Grant had been commissioned in the First Royal Tank Regiment. I was delighted that a third generation of the Oliver family was serving in the forces of the Queen. He is now a Lt Colonel and is enjoying army life as much as his father did.